The Accessibility Imperative

Implications of the Convention on the Rights of Persons with Disabilities for Information and Communication Technologies

Edited by G3ict
The Global Initiative for Inclusive ICTs
October 2007

The Accessibility Imperative is published by G3ict, a Division of the Wireless Internet Institute (W2i) and World Times, Inc., to build on the momentum set by the first G3ict Global Forum, co-hosted by the Global Alliance for ICT and Development and the Secretariat for the Convention on the Rights of Persons with Disabilities, at United Nations Headquarters in New York on March 26, 2007.

This reference document serves as a basis for seminars and roundtable discussions around the world in the context of the G3ict initiative and provides a multi-annual living knowledge base with ongoing updates in both electronic and printed form.

Funding of G3ict programs is provided by:
IBM Corporation, Air France, W2i, Internet Speech, VEMICS, NIIT, The Mozilla Foundation Samsung

Co-Hosts of G3ict Workshops in 2007-2008 as of this publication include: the United Nations Secretariat for the Convention on the Rights of Persons with Disabilities, the United Nations Global Alliance for ICT and Development, the International Telecommunications Union, the Honorable Daniel Scioli, Vice President of the Republic of Argentina, the Korea Agency for Digital Opportunity and Promotion (KADO), Politecnico di Milano, CIFAL Atlanta (DCP UNITAR), the City of Chicago, the Wireless Internet Institute, the Digital Inclusion Forum, TechShare and the Royal National Institute for the Blind.

ISBN 978-0-6151-7608-6

G3ict

A flagship partnership initiative of GAID, the United Nations Global Alliance for ICT and Development, G3ict was launched on December 4, 2006 with the support of W2i, the Wireless Internet Institute, in cooperation with GAID and the Secretariat for the Convention on the Protection and Promotion of the Rights and Dignity of Persons with Disabilities.

This book has been made possible thanks to the generous contributions of the following organizations:

Principal Book Sponsor

Book Sponsors

Program Sponsors and Co-Hosts

CONTENTS

OPENING REMARKS BY MR. BAN KI-MOON 7
SECRETARY GENERAL OF THE UNITED NATIONS 7
FOREWORD 9
ACKNOWLEDGEMENTS 12

THE CONVENTION FOR THE RIGHTS OF PERSONS WITH DISABILITIES...15

THE G3ICT INITIATIVE: IMPLEMENTING THE RESOLUTIONS OF THE WORLD SUMMIT ON THE INFORMATION SOCIETY AND THE MILLENNIUM DEVELOPMENT GOALS 16
FOSTERING UNIVERSAL RULES FOR ICT ACCESSIBILITY 21
OVERVIEW OF THE NEW CONVENTION ON THE RIGHTS OF PERSONS WITH DISABILITIES AND ITS IMPLICATIONS FOR ICTS...23

PROMOTING ACCESSIBLE INFORMATION AND COMMUNICATION TECHNOLOGIES FOR PERSONS WITH DISABILITIES...27

FROM DIGITAL DIVIDE TO DIGITAL DIVERSITY: THE IMPERATIVE FOR INCLUSIVE INFORMATION AND COMMUNICATION TECHNOLOGIES 28
AT A GLANCE: THE DEMOGRAPHIC IMPERATIVE OF ACCESSIBILITY 35
ASSESSING THE ACCESSIBILITY OF ICT PRODUCTS 41

SUCCESS STORIES: HARNESSING THE POWER OF ACCESSIBLE AND ASSISTIVE INFORMATION AND COMMUNICATIONS TECHNOLOGIES 49

TELEWORK: OPENING NEW EMPLOYMENT OPPORTUNITIES FOR PERSONS WITH DISABILITIES 50
POETA: FIGHTING EXCLUSION IN THE AMERICAS WITH ASSISTIVE AND ACCESSIBLE TECHNOLOGIES 57
MAKING ACCESSIBILITY WORK FOR ALL IN EDUCATION 60
ASSISTING SELF-EXPRESSION WITH TECHNOLOGY: THE YONSEI REHABILITATION SCHOOL EXPERIENCE...66
ACCESSIBLE EDUCATION FOR PEOPLE WITH SPECIAL NEEDS AS THE BASIS FOR CREATING AN OPEN INFORMATION SOCIETY 72
LEVELING THE PLAYING FIELD AND CHANGING WHAT IT MEANS TO BE BLIND 77
WEB ACCESSIBILITY AT GENERAL ELECTRIC 91

CORE CHALLENGES AND OPPORTUNITIES FOR INDUSTRY AND THE PRIVATE SECTOR 97

NEW DIRECTIONS FOR ACCESSIBLE AND ASSISTIVE INFORMATION AND COMMUNICATIONS TECHNOLOGIES..98
ACCESSIBILITY AND BUSINESS VALUE 105

THE MISSING LINK: FINANCING THE INDUSTRY 108
ANATOMY OF AN INDUSTRY SUCCESS STORY: JAWS 113
ACCESSIBILITY CHALLENGES AND OPPORTUNITIES OVER THE WEB.......... 116
OPEN AND ACCESSIBLE: NEW MODELS FOR COLLABORATIVE INNOVATION
.... 121
INTERNET FOR EVERYONE: CONSUMERS, BUSINESSES, AND GOVERNMENTS
.... 125
PUBLIC-PRIVATE PARTNERSHIPS: THE EUROPEAN PROJECT ASK-IT 131

**HARMONIZATION AND STANDARDIZATION: OPPORTUNITIES
FOR PERSONS WITH DISABILITIES AND THE PRIVATE SECTOR
.... 137**

EUROPEAN DISABILITY STRATEGY AND ACCESSIBILITY 138
ACCESSIBILITY STANDARDS FOR INFORMATION AND COMMUNICATIONS
TECHNOLOGIES: THE JAPANESE EXPERIENCE.. 145
THE IMPORTANCE OF HARMONIZATION: PERSPECTIVES FROM THE
INFORMATION TECHNOLOGY INDUSTRY COUNCIL 149
MEDIA LEADING THE PATH TO PROVIDING ACCESSIBLE INFORMATION AND
DEPLOYING HARMONIZATION AND REGULATIONS 153
THE WORLD WIDE WEB CONSORTIUM ACCESSIBILITY INITIATIVE 161
CONSUMERS AND ACCESSIBILITY STANDARDS: THE EUROPEAN PERSPECTIVE
.... 166

**HOW CAN LEGISLATORS AND REGULATORS FOSTER
INNOVATION, HARMONIZATION AND COMPLIANCE................. 169**

ICTS AND PARLIAMENTS: OPPORTUNITIES TO FOSTER LEGISLATION
SUPPORTING ACCESSIBILITY 170
LEGISLATION AS A TOOL TO IMPLEMENT ACCESSIBILITY REQUIREMENTS 176
ESTABLISHING ACCESSIBILITY STANDARDS THROUGH LEGISLATION AND
REGULATION: THE EXPERIENCE OF THE UNITED STATES ACCESS BOARD. 181
ENFORCING ICT ACCESSIBILITY RULES 186
LEGISLATIVE DEVELOPMENTS: NEW OPPORTUNITIES FOR THE DISABILITY
MOVEMENT 194
CRITICAL ISSUES FOR DEVELOPING COUNTRIES IN IMPLEMENTING THE
CONVENTION ON THE RIGHTS OF PERSONS WITH DISABILITIES 198
SOUTH AFRICA: PARLIAMENTARY LIFE AND ACCESSIBILITY 205
AN OVERVIEW OF THE RATIFICATION AND IMPLEMENTATION PROCESS OF
THE CONVENTION ON THE RIGHTS OF PERSONS WITH DISABILITIES 210

**BEST PRACTICES COMPENDIUM: A RESOURCE GUIDE TO
ACCESSIBLE AND ASSISTIVE ICT APPLICATIONS 215**

AABAC... *217*
AccessAbill *218*
Access Israel.. *219*
Adaptive Multiple Information System *220*
Adaptive Technology Center for the Blind *221*

Archimedes *222*
ASK-IT *223*
Assistive Robot Service Manipulator *224*
BIME – Bath Institute of Medical Engineering *225*
BlueEar *226*
BlueIRIS *227*
Bobby *228*
"Breaking Down Barriers" International Film Festival *229*
DAISY *230*
Deaf Alerter *231*
Deafblind *232*
DIADEM *233*
Disabilityart.com *234*
EZ Access *235*
Full Access through Technology *236*
GameON! *237*
Geographic Area: Europe *237*
House of Windows *238*
MATILDAH *239*
Mobile Care *240*
Mugunghwa Electronics *241*
National Accessibility Portal – South Africa *242*
Neater Eater *243*
PEBBLES – Bringing Learning Environments to Students .. *244*
PEN-International *245*
POETA *246*
Geographic Area: Latin America *246*
RoboBraille *247*
Royal National Institute for the Blind *248*
Sightsavers Dolphin Pen *249*
Stimulation and Therapeutic Activity Center *250*
Talking Tins *251*
T-Base Communications with Vision Australia *252*
The Signing Web Project *253*
Trekker *254*
Trinity College of Music *255*
Wheelchairnet.org *256*
WiseDX *257*
WWAAC - World-Wide Augmentative & Alternative Communication *258*

APPENDIX **259**

CONVENTION ON THE RIGHTS OF PERSONS WITH DISABILITIES 259
LIST OF SIGNATORY STATES OF THE CONVENTION ON THE RIGHTS OF
PERSONS WITH DISABILITIES 287

INDEX **289**

Opening Remarks by Mr. Ban Ki-Moon

Secretary General of the United Nations

*Excerpts from remarks at the opening session of the meeting of the
Steering Committee of the Global Alliance for Information and
Communication Technologies and Development,*
Santa Clara, California, February 27, 2007

"Information and communications technologies have a central role to play in the quest for development, dignity and peace. The international consensus on this point is clear. We saw it at the 2000 Millennium Summit and at the 2005 World Summit. And we saw it in the two phases of the World Summit on the Information Society. With the launch of the Global Alliance for ICT and Development last March, the international community has taken that consensus a crucial step further".

"It is important that you work as a true partnership of all essential stakeholders -- governments, civil society, the private sector, academia and others. All of you are needed if we are to succeed.

So let us use all our energy and innovation to harness ICT to our work towards the Millennium Development Goals. Let us turn the digital divide into digital opportunity. Let us promote new business models, public policies and technology solutions in the global approach to development.

The United Nations family is a willing and able partner in that process.

I send you my best wishes for a successful meeting, and look forward to learning about your progress".

Foreword

The "Accessibility Imperative" is the first attempt to publish a comprehensive overview of the implications of the dispositions of the Convention on the Rights of Persons with Disabilities for ICTs – Information and Communications Technologies.

Out of 34 non-procedural articles of the Convention, 14 contain specific ICT-related dispositions, which cover accessibility mandates for both the public and private sectors. ICT applications addressed include employment, education, media, and government services. States are also required to promote and support the development of affordable assistive technologies and to foster better ICT product development methods, namely by promoting universal design and development cycles which incorporate accessibility specifications at an early stage of product design.

The implications of these dispositions, once translated into local legislations and regulations, are considerable, especially in the context of ICT markets driven by global standards.

On March 26, 2007, G3ict, the Global Initiative for Inclusive ICTs, a Flagship Advocacy Initiative of the United Nations Global Alliance for ICT and Development, convened 175 leaders representing persons living with disabilities, ICT vendors and users, government agencies, and international development institutions at UN headquarters to offer key perspectives and engage in a critical dialogue.

The following chapters were derived from the proceedings of this meeting, as well as from subsequent workshops held in Russia, South Korea, and the United States. After a brief overview of the Convention, the main sections of the book are organized within the four principal areas of inquiry assigned to G3ict by its Steering Committee:

1 Sharing best practices for accessible and assistive ICT solutions
2 Exploring core areas of opportunity for ICT applications for persons living with disabilities
3 Promoting standardization and harmonization of accessible and inclusive ICT solutions
4 Documenting legislative and regulatory resources and references

These core chapters are then followed by a case study compendium and the full text of the Convention on the Rights of Persons with Disabilities.

Beyond the wealth of information and experience gathered, one important outcome of this first dialogue is the strong consensus which emerged among all stakeholders on fundamental issues and directions for the future.

Consensus on the scope of the challenges to be tackle:
- The acceleration and pervasive usage of ICT applications in all aspects of contemporary society make ensuring their accessibility for persons living with disabilities indispensable.
- The acceleration of innovation tends to create a growing accessibility gap in all ICT areas.
- While new ICT based assistive technologies bring unprecedented opportunities for persons living with disabilities, innovators lack funding and the industry remains very fragmented.

Consensus on directions for industry:
- Agreed upon standards are a prerequisite to lowering costs through mass production, increased competition, and innovation.
- Standardization success stories, such as the W3C WAI initiative or closed captioning for TV, demonstrate the feasibility of effective public-private coordination in major application areas.
- Developing greater accessibility for ICT products and services should be good business, given market demographics and the fact that accessibility benefits a large population beyond persons with disabilities themselves.

Consensus on steps for governments:
- Public procurement is a natural avenue to promote accessibility and standards by leveraging government ICT applications and purchasing power.
- Alignment of national legislation and regulations with the dispositions of the Convention will create a favorable environment to fostering accessible and assistive ICTs.
- However, national legislation and regulations should ultimately support global standards and carefully avoid fragmenting the market

which would hinder the potential to lower the cost of accessible and assistive ICTs for persons living with disabilities.

Consensus on international cooperation:
- International cooperation in matters of accessibility are occurring among representatives of the largest ICT markets in the context of various standardization organizations covering different types of technology and should be encouraged.
- Sharing best practices and effective solutions among all stakeholders should be promoted as an important market development factor and a practical source to determine "reasonable accommodation."
- Issues specific to the situation of developing nations need particular attention.

The results of this dialogue were most helpful to further refine the priorities and action plans for G3ict. In 2007 and 2008, the Initiative will continue to promote a continuous dialogue among all stakeholders around the world.

As G3ict pursues those endeavors, the active participation and support of leading representatives of persons living with disabilities alongside industry, government, and large ICT users from the private and public sectors continue to bring unique strengths to its inquiry. Our sincere appreciation goes to the many individuals and organizations who have made G3ict such a high-energy, purposeful, and far-reaching initiative.

Axel Leblois
Executive Director, G3ict
October 2007

Acknowledgements

As an Advocacy Initiative, the overall success of G3ict, including the content generated for The Accessibility Imperative, is entirely dependent on strategic partnerships formed with engaged participants in both the public and private sectors. G3ict would thus like to acknowledge a number of organizations and individuals for their ongoing support of the initiative and for their subsequent contributions to this book.

Firstly, G3ict would like to thank its main partners at the United Nations: the Global Alliance for ICT and Development (GAID) and the Secretariat for the Convention on the Rights of Persons with Disabilities for their constant support and invaluable guidance and feedback. G3ict also wishes to extend its appreciation to **Ambassador Luis Gallegos,** *G3ict Program Chair, Former Chair of the Ad Hoc Committee on the Convention on the Rights of Persons with Disabilities and Ambassador of Ecuador to the United States, for his constant generosity, encouragement, and support of the initiative since its inception. G3ict is also most appreciative of the contributions of its workgroup chairs:* **CN Madhusudan** *President of NIIT Ventures,* **John Vaughn** *Chairman of the Board of the National Council on Disability,* **Inmaculada Placencia Porrero** *Directorate General for Employment, Social Affairs, and Equal Opportunities of the European Commission, and* **Marcel Boisard**, *former Assistant Secretary General of the United Nations and Executive Director of UNITAR, the United Nations Institute for Training and Research.*

G3ict would also like to recognize co-hosting institutions: the Wireless Internet Institute, the Korea Agency for Digital Opportunity and Promotion (KADO), Techshare, and Politecnico di Milano for hosting key meetings and playing an active role in the development of future activities. In addition, G3ict acknowledges the following partner organizations for their generous input and participation over the past year: the International Telecommunications Union (ITU), the Inter-Parliamentary Union (IPU), the National Council on Disability (NCD), the European Commission, the Korea Agency for Digital Opportunity, the Organization of American States and the Shepherd Center.

G3ict is especially appreciative of the overarching support that it has received from its official sponsors: IBM, NIIT, Air France, the Wireless Internet Institute (W2i), Vemics, CIFAL Atlanta (UNITAR DCP), and Internet Speech, without whom G3ict's 2007 activities, including The Accessibility Imperative, would not have been possible.

A special note of sincere appreciation also goes to **Frances West** *and* **Anne-Rivers Forcke** *for their programmatic contributions and support on behalf of IBM, to* **Alex Mejia** *for his commitment to ensure the full participation of local governments and CIFAL Atlanta to G3ict and to* **Daniel Aghion**, *Executive Director and co-Founder of the Wireless Internet Institute, for his thought leadership and many years of dedication to promote solutions to bridge the Digital Divide around the world..*

Most importantly, G3ict wishes to acknowledge the contributing authors of The Accessibility Imperative for their invaluable contributions to the book and to the initiative on the whole:

Tamas Babinszki – *Accessibility and Section 508 Consultant/Assistive Technology Analyst, Project Performance Corporation and the U.S. Patent and Trademark Office, Overbrook International Program Alumnus*
Peter Blanck – *University Professor & Chairman of the Burton Blatt Institute at Syracuse University, Co-Director of the University of Trondheim e-Accessibility Project*
Judy Brewer – *Director of the Web Accessibility Initiative, The World Wide Web Consortium (W3C)*
Larry Campbell – *Administrator, Overbrook International Program*
Timothy Creagan *Senior Accessibility Specialist, Technical and Information Services, Access Board, United States*
Anda Filip – *Ambassador, Inter-Parliamentary Union*
Barry Fingerhut – *General Partner, Synconium Partners*
Nikolaos Floratos – *Project Dissemination Leader, e-ISOTIS*
Anne-Rivers Forcke – *IBM Human Ability and Accessibility Center*
Luis Gallegos– *Ambassador of Ecuador to the United States, Chairman, G3ict, Former Chair of the Ad Hoc Committee for a Comprehensive and Integral International Convention on the Protection and Promotion of the Rights and Dignity of Persons with Disabilities*
Chiara Giovannini – *Program Manager, European Association Representing Consumers in Standardization (ANEC)*
Larry Goldberg – *Director, Media Access, WGBH Boston*
Jean-Pierre Gonnot – *Chief, Secretariat for the Convention on the Rights of Persons with Disabilities*
Martin Gould – *Director of Research and Technology, National Council on Disability*
Frank Hecker – *Executive Director, Mozilla Foundation*
Ted Henter – *Director, Henter Math*
 Creator of Jaws, Freedom Scientific
Hendrietta Ipeleng Bogopane-Zulu *Member of the South African Parliament, National Assembly, Chairperson of the South African Delegation to the Preparatory Commission of the Convention on the Rights of Persons with Disabilities*
Emdad Khan – *Founder, President & CEO, Internet Speech*

Sarbuland Khan – *Executive Coordinator, Global Alliance for ICT and Development*
Boris Kotsik – *Director, UNESCO Institute for Information Technologies in Education*
Preety Kumar – *Founder, President and CEO, Deque Systems, Inc*
Axel Leblois – *Executive Director and Founder, G3ict*
René Léon – *Program Manager, POETA, Organization of American States*
Dipendra Manocha – *Assistant Project Manager, DAISY for All Project, DAISY Consortium, Honorary Director IT and Services, National Association for the Blind, New Delhi, India*
Emilie McCabe – *General Manager, IBM Global Public Sector*
Ilene Morris-Sambur – *Founder and CEO, Coraworks*
Michael Paciello – *Founder and Principal, The Paciello Group*
SukJa Park – *Principal, Yonsei Rehabilitation School, Korea*
Inmaculada Placencia Porrero – *European Commission Directorate General Employment, Social Affairs, and Equal Opportunities*
Steven Rothstein – *President, Perkins School for the Blind*
Ken Salaets – *Executive Director of Access Standards and Director of Government Relations, Information Technology Industry Council*
Natalia Tokareva – *Project Manager, UNESCO Institute for Information Technologies in Education*
Victor Tsaran – *Accessibility Program Manager, Yahoo Corporation*
Yannis Vardakastanis – *President, European Disability Forum*
Hajime Yamada – *Toyo University, Japan, Chair of the Standardization Investigation Committee for Improvement of Accessibility Common to Areas of Information Technology and Software Products*

Finally, G3ict would like to express its gratitude to its hard-working team of dedicated research analysts and editors: **Pauley Tedoff**, *G3ict Program Manager and Lead Editor for "The Accessibility Imperative", whose energy and dedication have made this project come to fruition, and* **Meagan Clem, Melissa Scholz** *and* **Emilie Pechar** *for their patient and efficient editorial work.*

The Convention for the Rights of Persons with Disabilities

Implications for Information and Communication Technologies

"Perhaps no other field allows for the inclusion of persons with disabilities into society as do ICTs"

Mr. Sha Zukang, United Nations Under Secretary-General, Department of Economic and Social Affairs

The G3ict Initiative: Implementing the Resolutions of the World Summit on the Information Society and the Millennium Development Goals

By Sarbuland Khan
Executive Coordinator, Global Alliance for ICT and Development

The rights of persons living with disabilities, including the right to accessible ICTs, are a fundamental aspect of Human Rights that many governments, NGOs, and the United Nations have been working on under the leadership of our colleagues of the Secretariat for the Convention on the Rights of Persons with Disabilities and of Ambassador Luis Gallegos who was the first Chair of the Ad Hoc Committee for the Convention on the Rights of Persons with Disabilities.

G3ict, the Global Initiative for Inclusive Information and Communication Technologies, embodies the commitment of the United Nations and the Global Alliance for ICT and Development to foster inclusive information technologies that serve to empower all individuals in society, including those with disabilities.

Inclusive ICTs and the
World Summit on the Information Society

Focusing on and addressing disability issues within the context of the information society was recognized by leading international organizations, governments, the private sector, civil society, and NGOs, as well as by a number of other stakeholders during the Geneva and Tunis Summits.

As reflected in the Geneva Principle, the world community committed to building the information society to pay, and I quote, "particular attention to the special needs of marginalized and vulnerable groups of society, including migrants, internally displaced persons and refugees, unemployed and underprivileged people, minorities, and nomadic people. We shall also recognize the special needs of older persons and persons with disabilities."

This excerpt is taken from the principles adopted by the Geneva Summit. The Geneva Plan of Action also addresses special requirements for underserved groups, including persons with disabilities, through appropriate educational and legislative measures, to ensure full inclusion in society. The Plan specifically emphasizes the need for research and development endeavors in achieving accessibility to information and knowledge for all.

The commitment to promoting the welfare of persons with disabilities was renewed during the Tunis Summit in 2005. The International Committee vowed to promote universal, equitable, and assistive technology for all people – especially those with disabilities – to ensure that benefits are more evenly distributed within society and that the digital divide is bridged through appropriate development opportunities.

Those participating in the Summit also specifically reaffirmed the need to meet the goals established by the Geneva Plan of Action and emphasized the imperative of developing ICTs that are accessible to all persons, including those with disabilities. In this context, special attention was given to universal design concepts and to assistive technologies that promote access to persons with disabilities.

Clearly, there was very broad, formal, and clear international consensus established by both the Geneva and Tunis Summits at the highest level of government and with the full participation of the private and public sectors. It is equally important to review how the objectives of G3ict relate to the Millennium Development Goals.

Inclusive ICTs and the Millennium Development Goals

There are two key elements in the Millennium Development Goals. One is to reduce the number of persons living in poverty by half by 2015, and the other is to reach out to the underserved, marginalized groups who do not have access to information technology.

Persons with disabilities are entitled to the same rights and opportunities as all other human beings. Not withstanding society's best intentions, however, the reality is that persons with disabilities face significant obstacles when it comes to full and equitable participation in society. Faced with existing physical and social barriers, such individuals are often excluded from their communities, often experiencing extreme alienation and isolation.

There are more than 650 million people in the world, at least 10% of the population in most countries, who live with disabilities. In most countries, one out of ten citizens has a physical, mental or sensory impairment. Exacerbating the situation is the fact that 80% of all persons with disabilities living in the developing world live in poor conditions. Clearly, development programs and strategies that integrate ICT should attempt to include disability issues in order to succeed. While the Millennium Development Goals do not make direct reference to persons with disabilities, achieving these goals with inclusive ICT applications will have a profound implication on the welfare of persons with disabilities.

For example, Goal 1 is to eradicate extreme poverty. Over 480 million persons with disabilities live in the developing world, and the number of persons with disabilities continues to increase due to unfavorable conditions of hunger, malnutrition, and poverty.

Goal 2 is to achieve universal primary education. According to UNESCO, only 1% to 2% of children with disabilities who live in a developing country receive education. According to UNFPA (United Nations Population Fund), around 20 million women a year acquire a disability as a result of complications during pregnancy and childbirth. Likewise, abnormal prenatal circumstances have been identified as one of the leading causes of disability in children, particularly in a developing country.

Goal 8 calls for developing a global partnership for development. Clearly, this is a need whose satisfaction is indispensable for the fulfillment of all the other goals. Developing a global partnership for development, particularly in the area of ICT development, is the underlying principle behind the establishment of the Global Alliance for ICT and Development.

As we know, G3ict has been launched as an advocacy partnership initiative of the Global Alliance for ICT and Development. I do not have the intention of describing the Alliance itself in detail. However, I would just like to state that G3ict exemplifies the type of programs that the Alliance supports. Most notably, G3ict operates as an effective global network of willing partners from industry, NGOs, international institutions, and governments – all coming from many different horizons with shared objectives.

G3ict is a significant step forward in the fulfillment of the commitments of the World Summit on the Information Society and of the United Nations Millennium Development Goals. Furthermore, the Initiative serves to foster the rapid implementation of the dispositions of the Convention on the Rights of Persons with Disabilities that specifically address equal access to ICTs. G3ict is a practical answer to empowering and further integrating persons with disabilities into society by leveraging accessible and assistive ICT solutions.

Fostering Universal Rules for ICT Accessibility

By Ambassador Luis Gallegos of Ecuador
Former Chair of the Ad Hoc Committee for a Comprehensive and
Integral International Convention on the Protection and Promotion of
the Rights and Dignity of Persons with Disabilities

It is an honor and a distinct pleasure to be a part of the Global Initiative for Inclusive Information and Communication Technologies. The Initiative will serve as an interactive venue for stakeholders and leading experts from around the world to come together to create, cultivate, reach consensus, and set direction for the future of accessible communication and information technologies for persons with disabilities.

We met at the United Nations in New York at the dawn of a historic week on the 30th of March, wherein the nations of the world had been invoked to sign the Convention on the Rights of Persons with Disabilities (hereafter referred to as the Convention), the first human rights convention of this millennium and the 8th Universal Convention on Human Rights.

A person is born with a disability or can acquire it by accident, sickness, or war. We must foresee that, as the world ages, disability will increase. The 650 million persons with disabilities will become more rather than less.

The Convention is an enforceable international instrument that will permit the nations of the world to meet the challenge that history has put before us to become a society in which all members, including the most vulnerable, can integrate and make a significant contribution.

Amidst diversity, we will find ourselves as members of a holistic society. The negotiation of the Convention proves that the emergence of a disability movement, supported by all stakeholders, can be a formidable force in civil society to foster the development of universal rules.

Article 9 of the Convention serves as the official guideline for accessibility, and it is my strong belief that G3ict will enable us all to challenge present reality in the rigorous pursuit of its implementation worldwide. I greatly admire and appreciate all those who work to promote the rights of persons with disabilities, as they are the stakeholders of a vital movement that is changing society and the world.

Overview of the New Convention on the Rights of Persons with Disabilities and Its Implications for ICTs

By Jean-Pierre Gonnot
Chief, Secretariat for the Convention on the Rights of Persons with Disabilities

On the 13th of December 2006, the United Nations General Assembly adopted the Convention on the Rights of Persons with Disabilities. The opening of the Convention for signature on March 30, 2007 was the first step toward ratification of entry into force. Countries have rushed to complete the domestic process that allowed them to begin signing the Convention and express their support and commitment towards complying with its principles. The Convention on the Rights of Persons with Disabilities, as Ambassador Luis Gallegos mentioned in his introductory remarks, is the eighth Human Rights Treaty agreed upon by the international community since the Universal Declaration of Human Rights in 1948. The adoption of such an instrument is therefore not "business as usual," but rather carries historical significance.

The new convention aims at ensuring that persons with disabilities enjoy the same human rights as everyone else and that they are able to live their lives as fully-fledged citizens who can make valuable contributions to society, if given the same opportunity as others. Despite theoretically being entitled to the entire range of civil, cultural, economic, political, and social rights that pertain to every human being, persons with disabilities are still deprived of most of these rights and discriminated against across the world. In essence, they continue to be primarily viewed as recipients of welfare or medical treatment, rather than as owners of pride.

The living conditions of persons with disabilities are also an unfortunate example of an overlooked developmental challenge. There are approximately half a billion persons with disabilities living amongst the poorest of the poor. Together with their family members, these are two billion people for whom disability is part of their daily lives. It is becoming increasingly clear that without addressing the reality of disability, it will be impossible to achieve Millennium Development Goals 1 and 2, which call for global poverty and hunger to be reduced by half and for universal primary education to be provided to all children by the year 2015, respectively.

The Convention is the principle and acting response to this dual human rights and developmental challenge. It clarifies and qualifies how all categories apply to all persons with disabilities. Furthermore, it identifies areas where adaptation should be made to enable persons with disabilities to effectively exercise their rights, as well as areas where their rights have been violated and thus where protection of such rights must be reinforced.

The Convention provides a set of eight fundamental principles, which serve as the basis for any legislative or policy-making action. I wish to focus, in particular, on two principles that have great relevance to G3ict, the Global Initiative for Inclusive Information and Communication Technologies: non-discrimination and accessibility.

Non-discrimination is a fundamental principle for human rights law that recognizes that every human being should be able to enjoy the same benefits and possess the same common basis for demanding equal human rights and associated freedoms. As for discrimination on the basis of disability, the Convention clearly states that civil society is responsible for ensuring that appropriate modifications are made to allow an individual with a disability to enjoy and exercise those same fundamental rights. The failure to provide such accommodation within the realm of what can be considered reasonable constitutes discrimination on the part of the state or society at hand. To this extent, the provision of accommodations for persons with disabilities rests in assuring equal access to building services, education, work, and information, among others.

Accessibility: the Convention on the Rights of Persons with Disabilities is the first human rights treaty made relevant to accessibility. According to Article 9, the state must ensure that private entities offering facilities and services to the public take into account the accessibility of those services. Perhaps, even more striking is the reference in Article 21 to freedom of expression and opinion within the private sector, which asserts, "the state must urge private entities that provide services to the general public, including through the Internet, to provide information and services in accessible and usable formats for persons with disabilities." The Convention clearly recognizes the role of the private sector in the field of information and communication technologies and points to its responsibility; however, it does not specify a direct obligation for the private sector in opening the door for socially responsible corporate initiatives. The Secretariat for the Convention believes that orientating the private sector towards such aspects of the Convention provides a unique opportunity for positive thinking and actions that can have a tremendous affect on the lives of persons with disabilities.

Promoting Accessible Information and Communication Technologies for Persons with Disabilities

From Digital Divide to Digital Diversity: The Imperative for Inclusive Information and Communication Technologies

Keynote Address at the First G3ict Global Forum by Emilie McCabe, General Manager, IBM Global Public Sector

It is an honor for me to be here today at the first G3ict Global Forum and to be with all of you who have personally embraced the need to make progress in meeting the need of accessibility. I am also proud to represent IBM, an enterprise that has truly embraced accessibility and inclusion for more than 90 years.

To get started, I would like to talk about the definition of accessibility. In order to do so, I will refer to an artifact from this new Internet-based information paradigm called Wikipedia. Wikipedia is actually a free-content, multilingual, online encyclopedia that has been created through the collaboration of contributors all around the world. The site itself is called a "wiki," which means that anyone can read or add articles. According to Wikipedia, the definition of accessibility is the degree to which a system is usable by as many people as possible and, more specifically, by persons with disabilities. As the Wikipedia definition suggests, accessibility is about providing equal access to everyone. IBM extends the definition one step further; we believe accessibility is about enabling human capability through innovation so that everyone can maximize their potential, regardless of age or ability.

At IBM, we see a continuum when we consider human abilities. Traditionally, disabilities have been viewed through a medical lens and include impairments to vision and hearing, as well as mobility and dexterity. What we have learned about human ability at IBM has led us to look at ways in which accessibility can help remove barriers and benefit a number of other communities in ways that have the potential for tremendous impact socially, economically, and politically.

First, let's consider the aging of our global population. This large population – many of whom were born in the years following World War II and are now in their 50s – is also referred to as the "baby boom generation." Based on the latest statistics, we know that:

1. By the year 2025, it is expected that more than 20% of the population of industrialized nations will be over the age of 60.

2. In the case of Australia, the number of individuals between the ages of 60 and 64 is expected to double over the next 10 years.

3. Likewise, in Japan, it is expected that 26% of the population will be over the age of 65 within the next 10 years.

4. And in China, 28% of the population is estimated to be 60 years of age or older by the year 2040 – that's compared with only 11% today.

The impact of this maturing population on various aspects of society is potentially profound. Let's look, for instance, at the area of employment: In the year 2000, it was estimated that, while 22 million Italian citizens were receiving pension, only 21 million were actually in the work force. When we think about the baby boom generation in the United States, the expectation is that by the year 2020, 50% of the US work force will be age 55 or over. The bottom line is this: As people age, they have a higher probability of developing a disability. With this in mind, we predict that accessible information technology (IT) solutions will become even more of a focus in the coming years.

A second community to consider is those people who may be uncomfortable or reluctant to use computers or other information technology. Assistive technologies (ATs) and principles of accessible design can be used to simplify and streamline user interfaces, helping to make technology easier to understand and less intimidating to use.

And third, we know that accessible IT can benefit those who are challenged with below-basic levels of literacy, or those people living in a region or nation where they don't speak the native language very well, or even at all. Clearly, what we have learned about removing barriers to using IT for persons with what we think of as "traditional disabilities" can be applied to benefit many different kinds of technology users.

But let's bring our attention back to the community at the nucleus of the accessibility discussion: persons with disabilities. The World Health Organization reports that there are between 750 million and one billion persons with disabilities around the globe.[1] They represent a skilled, experienced, and diverse employee pool, an active and participative constituency, and a market opportunity. If we consider the purchasing power of this community in the United States *alone*, we see that persons with disabilities represent about US $225 billion of disposable income, making a strong argument in support of accessibility.

For many organizations and individuals, accessibility started as a philanthropic effort, but gradually those motivations changed due to a number of forces. Clearly, legislative and government forces – and by those I mean social, procurement, and employment – have had

---

[1] According to Baseline Assessment Inclusion and Disability in World Bank Activities Report – June 2002

significant influence on the accessibility movement. These motivations are changing globally and perhaps are best expressed in terms of business value. For example, the Internet has had a tremendous impact on how businesses and governments view accessibility. As a delivery channel, the Internet has exponentially increased consumer choice, enabling people to change vendors or service providers with the click of the mouse. This seemingly endless array of options and choices has disrupted established business assumptions about customer loyalty and renewed the focus on creating a personal and unique customer experience. For businesses worldwide, providing accessible online information and consumer services is the first and most basic requirement for generating customer satisfaction. Interestingly enough, "consumers" in the commercial sector are "constituents" in the public sector, and consumers' changing expectations for commercial information and services have led to evolving expectations for information and services in the public sector, re-enforcing the need for more easily accessible government information and services.

Moreover, we must take into consideration the fact that organizations make significant investments in information technology and other services. How well those technologies are used or adopted – and, therefore, the financial investment in those systems – is certainly going to be impacted by the degree to which users' experiences are positive and productive.

We believe that accessibility is not simply a result of good design, but that it is equally about improving the quality of the information and communication technology such that it improves the quality of our lives. That being said, I wish to share with you how IBM, as a private-sector enterprise, has participated in the accessibility movement. We are at once an employer and a provider of information technology and capability. Certainly, most private-sector companies face many of the same challenges that we do. As an employer, for example, we hired our first employee with a disability in the year 1914, and that was simply because our founder, Thomas J. Watson, believed that the most important thing was to hire the most talented, well-prepared person for the job. That philosophy lives on today and, as a result, we vigorously pursue diversity and accessibility through our "Global Work Force Diversity Initiative." And as a prospective employer we are focused on the need for more comprehensive academic courses and curricula to teach inclusive IT design.

As I mentioned earlier, as a provider of information technologies and capabilities, we have a long history of developing accessible technology – not just for our own use, but also for our clients. We developed the Braille printer in 1975 and a talking typewriter in 1980. We subsequently produced one of the best screen readers for the blind. In 1985, we established the IBM Human Ability and Accessibility Center, a worldwide organization that continues to support the development of technologies that assist persons with disabilities and the aging population. To this end, we have also established a corporate instruction that mandates that our hardware, software, services, and marketing materials are all accessible. The Human Ability and Accessibility Center reports on the accessibility status of IBM products, services and internal processes quarterly. Most recently we've created technology assets, like IBM Easy Web Browsing, which allows novice users, senior citizens, and persons with limited vision or eye fatigue to access Website information. As an innovator, we help our clients to enhance their market reach through the adoption of accessible Internet-based information, which among other positive effects, has the potential to both extend market reach to a broader set of communities and increase revenues. Furthermore, we leverage Web-based information systems to improve employee productivity through the use of accessible tools, which mitigate risk and provide a range of global accessibility benefits.

Many governments and businesses are just getting started on their path to accessibility transformation. Those who have already moved along this path have developed tested and proven principles that can guide new innovations in this process. One of the greatest values that we have observed organizations receiving from accessibility is the creation of customized tools that can be applied to constituents' individual needs. As such, we encourage our clients to allow the needs of the people who depend on their organization to shape their approach, rather than just their technology or legislation. We also remind them that a wonderful aspect of working with accessibility is that it allows a company or organization to serve its clients or beneficiaries while also serving itself. To this extent, it is one of the rare instances that we can truly deem a win-win opportunity.

There are many ways for those who have already made progress in the field of accessibility to share their thoughts and experiences with others. Wikipedia, which I mentioned earlier, is a great tool to share insight gained along the way. It is the basis for a process to collect and distribute human knowledge on a topic as critical as accessibility. Once progress is established and well-documented, it must be sustained. We encourage those institutions that have already moved through this process to make sure they find ways to continue in that capacity by working closely with other organizations, as well as with their constituents with disabilities. Accessibility is not a state to be achieved, but an ongoing process that must be nurtured, shared, and sustained. To succeed as a global community, we must work together.

Finally, I would ask that you remember that accessibility is not about serving the needs of one segment of the population. It is really about the elimination of barriers. Accessible and inclusive IT solutions – whether in the form of new technology or new standards, new policies or new partnerships – are truly innovations that matter for the world.

At a Glance: The Demographic Imperative of Accessibility

By Anne-Rivers Forcke
IBM Human Ability and Accessibility Center

Over the course of the last thirty years, the rate at which information and communication technologies (ICTs) have "diffused" or permeated our daily lives and the rate at which we have adopted these technologies have both grown steadily. Considering the continued growth of the global population, as well as the ever-increasing use of information and communication technologies within emerging economies, the trends seem to point toward an ongoing global demand for ICT products and services. However, it is when we consider the growth in the global population and the growth in the global number of ICT users within the context of Article 9 of the Convention on the Rights of Persons with Disabilities and the recently-published *Measuring Disability Prevalence* (World Bank, March 2007), that these dramatically increasing rates of diffusion and adoption of technology help to crystallize the social, technical and commercial imperatives for the development of accessible ICT.

During the years 2001 – 2005, dramatic growth occurred in the number of information and communication technology (ICT) users worldwide. Globally, during this time, the population of fixed line and mobile phone subscribers nearly doubled, as illustrated in *Table 1*:

Telecommunications Users[2] - Population of fixed line and mobile phone subscribers (per 1,000 people in the population)	2001	2003	2005	Change 2001-2005
Global	326	406	552	69%
Low income countries	31	49	113	265%
Middle income countries	260	387	587	126%
High income countries	1171	1260	1337	14%

Table 1

The global rate at which Internet users grew was similar to the global growth in fixed and mobile phone subscribers. However, there was a dramatic growth in Internet users in low income countries, as highlighted in *Table 2*:

Internet Users[3] (per 1,000 people in the population)	2001	2003	2005	Change 2001-2005
Global	80	115	136	70%
Low income countries	5	16	44	780%
Middle income countries	35	73	114	226%
High income countries	378	460	523	38%

Table 2

Clearly, during these years, information and communication technologies not only diffused throughout countries of all income levels, but they were also embraced and adopted by end-users.

---

[2] World Bank Group, World Development Indicators, 2007
[3] *ibid.*

Global Population and Disabilities

The "medical model of disability" – the model most widely understood and interpreted today – considers disability "a physical, mental, or psychological condition that limits a person's activities," linked to various medical conditions and viewed as a problem residing solely in the affected individual. Considering this model of disability, along with statistics reported in both developed and developing countries, the World Bank estimated the number persons with disabilities (PWDs) to be between 10-12% of the global population.[4]

Year	2007	2010	2020	2030	2040	2050
Population[5] (in billions)	6.7	6.8	7.6	8.3	8.9	9.4
Estimates of global PWD population (imputed as 10-12%, in millions)	670-804	680-816	760-912	830-984	890-1,068	940-1,128

Table 3

Using the World Bank's estimates and based on a global population calculated at just over 6.7 billion people (as of September 2007), *Table 3* shows the estimated current global PWD population at just under a billion people (680-816 million people) today, with the population expected to exceed one billion (900 million – 1.1 billion) as we approach the midpoint of the 21st century.[6]

---

[4] Mont, D., *Measuring Disability Prevalence*, World Bank, March 2007
[5] US Census Bureau
[6] United Nations, Population Division of the Department of Economic and Social Affairs of the United Nations Secretariat, *World Population Prospects*: *The 2006 Revision,* September 2007

While our estimate of the world's population of persons with disabilities seems a relatively constant percentage (10-12%), the increase in the rate of growth of the over-65 population is expected to more than double over the next 40 years, climbing from 7 to 16% or more than 1.5 billion people globally, as shown in *Table 4*:

Year	2007	2010	2020	2025	2030	2040	2050
Population[7] (in billions)	6.7	6.8	7.6		8.3	8.9	9.4
Forecast of global population over age 65[8] (in millions)	469			760-830			1,504

Table 4

This aging population is significant in both its number and its implications for ICT development. As a person ages, the probability of losing some amount of functionality – whether it's hearing, vision, mobility, dexterity, or cognitive – increases significantly, creating an immediate "second tier" of demand for accessible ICT in the form of persons over 65 who lose sensory, motor, or cognitive capabilities.

Looking, then, through the lens of the medical model of disability, and considering almost exclusively the global populations of PWDs, plus those people aged 65 years and older and likely to have or develop a medical disability, there is today an estimated market force of *more than* one billion people worldwide who require that the information and

---

[7] *Ibid.*

[8] Haub, C., *2007 World Population Data Sheet,* and United Nations Population Division

communication technology – upon which they are increasingly dependent – be accessible.

A New Approach

While the medical model is the construct for disabilities that we are historically most accustomed to using, over time the international community has largely come to recognize that the medical model is not an effective or empowering conceptual framework for promoting the full inclusion of persons with disabilities in society.[9] As the paradigm of disabilities has shifted, it has moved away from the medical model and moved toward the social model.

Unlike the medical model of disability, the social model of disability views disability as "arising from the interaction of a person's functional status with the[10] physical, cultural, and policy environments." According to the social model, disability is the outcome of the interaction of a person with his or her environment and thus is neither person- nor environment-specific.[11] Within the social model, then, a disability results when a person attempts to communicate, yet does not understand or speak the national or local language. Similarly, a disability results when someone who has never before operated a phone or computer attempts to use one – with no success. In both cases, a disability has occurred, because the person was not able to interact with his or her environment.

---

[9] Guernsey, K. et al, *Making Inclusion Operational: Legal and Institutional Resources for World Bank Staff on the Inclusion of Disability Issues in Investment Projects*, World Bank, October 2006

[10] The general approach for defining such prevalence follows closely the UN Washington Group on Disability Statistics. The group's website can be found at http://www.cdc.gov/nchs/citygroup.htm

[11] Mont, D., *Measuring Disability Prevalence*, World Bank, March 2007

Compared to the medical model of disability, the social model of disability inevitably encompasses more of the global population in more situations and under more circumstances. As the global population grows and ages, and as it migrates and encounters new technologies, there are evermore opportunities for societal disabilities to result and an ever-greater imperative for accessible information and communication technologies that *enable* – not impede – the interactions between people and their environments.

Assessing the Accessibility of ICT Products

By Martin Gould
Director of Research and Technology, National Council on Disability

The National Council on Disability (NCD) is an independent federal agency whose overall purpose is to promote policies, programs, practices, and procedures that guarantee equal opportunity for all individuals with disabilities, regardless of the nature or severity of the disability. The Council seeks to empower individuals with disabilities to achieve economic self-sufficiency, independent living, inclusion, and integration into all aspects of society.

NCD is composed of 15 members appointed by the President and confirmed by the U.S. Senate. In its 1986 report *Toward Independence,* NCD first proposed that Congress should enact a civil rights law for persons with disabilities. In 1990, the Americans with Disabilities Act was signed into law. The following article serves to provide a brief overview of NCD's research on the accessibility of select IT products and assistive technologies. This overview will address results from our Design for Inclusion research study that involved: a User study, a Product analysis, an Industry analysis, and a Market analysis. I will also draw attention to the implications of these research findings for the global market and work of G3ict.

According to the 2006 report entitled "Digital Planet," the Global ICT Market Place is valued at $3 trillion. Digital Planet also projected that the Global ICT Marketplace would be valued at about $4 trillion by the year 2009. What is the world buying? According to the Digital Planet, in absolute dollars, communication is the largest

41

category among the four major ICT categories that have been determined as hardware, software, services, and communication – which accounts for $1.57 trillion out of a total of $3 trillion of total ICT spending.

In a design conclusion study conducted in 2004, we examined the roles and the perspectives of the industry, federal government, and consumers with respect to six product lines: Automated Teller Machines, Personal Digital Assistant (or the PDA), distance learning software, cell phones, televisions, and voice recognition technology. We also analyzed emerging ICT markets in the top five developing countries with the highest populations[12] as having the highest overall market potential: China, India, Russia, Mexico, and Turkey.

There were three major guiding questions used during our analysis:

1. Is there a market to develop more accessibility in the product?

2. Is there a need to improve design in each product line?

3. What factors influence the market for more accessibly designed products for each of the product lines presented?

The purpose was to document user acceptance and use of universally designed products. Five focus groups with participants with different disabilities were recruited. The groups discussed specific experiences with the six products, generated lists of product features that affect the accessibility of the devices, and rated the impact of each device's feature on the overall accessibility of the product based on a particular range of functional capabilities. The research study also analyzed the

---

[12]Source: GlobalEDGE (2003)

data which resulted in listed features that the consumers felt optimized the accessibility of the specific product line from a wider array of products represented.

We then analyzed the data from the focus groups, resulting in a list of features that maximize the accessibility of a specific product line for the range of functional limitations represented by this study. We also worked with focus groups to conduct performance testing to gain objective measurements. We gave participants brief evaluation scenarios in which they were asked to perform a series of typical tasks associated with each device. The ability of each participant to perform the task, as well as the degree to which an accessibility feature actually facilitated task performance was documented. The end result was to assign an accessibility grade to each product. It was our hope that the grading of the different products would prove useful to the designers and manufacturers of those products in helping to identify the accessibility features that should be considered during product design. The key findings of the user study were:

1. Users with disabilities are often asked to pay high prices for phones with feature sets that are not useful to them;

2. Rapid changes in technology often cause decreases in accessibility;

3. Users are reluctant to adopt technologies that have proven frustrating in the past;

4. Users have difficulty finding devices that match their functional capabilities due to the lack of knowledge and familiarity sales associates have with accessibility features;

5. Users are reluctant to invest in technologies that have an unproven accessibility record; and

6. Accessibility solutions must consider the needs of the individual with disabilities.

The grades and their respective definitions were:

A = Excellent accessibility. Users with an impairment are generally able to make full use of the product, with few limitations.

B = Good accessibility. Users with an impairment are generally able to make good use of the product, yet some areas of product functionality are not accessible.

C = Fair accessibility. Users with an impairment can access some of the functionality of the device, but many aspects of product functionality are not accessible.

D = Poor accessibility. Users with an impairment can make use of a small proportion of the functionality of a device, but most aspects of product functionality are not accessible.

F = Accessibility failure. Users with an impairment are generally not able to use the product.

Accessibility Grades for Each Target Population for the Six Product Lines

Target Population	Product Lines					
	ATMs	Cell Phones	Distance Learning Software	PDAs	TVs	Voice Recognition Software
Low Vision	C	C	C	C	B	C
Blind	D	F	F	F	D	D
Hard-of-Hearing	A	C	B	B	B	D
Deaf	A	D	D	B	B	F
Upper Mobility	C	C	C	D	A	A
Lower Mobility	C	A	A	A	A	A
Cognitive	C	C	C	C	A	C

As is evident from the results, certain product lines are very accessible to some persons with disabilities, while they are largely inaccessible to others. If one could establish a universal design process, the designer could consolidate the product based upon which product line received the greatest accessibility ratings.

It would also be helpful if designers were to consult the target populations during future product development for product lines that received accessibility grades of D or F. For example, in the case of ATMs, users who are blind will likely be unable to use an ATM or portions of its core functionality, due to the lack of accessibility features. As such, blind users should be considered in the design of new features for ATMs. In that same vein, cellular phones are largely inaccessible to users who are blind or deaf. Incorporating more features that make this product line more accessible to these users will expand the market for cellular telephony. Similarly, distance learning software is largely inaccessible to users who are blind or deaf. Adhering to accessibility regulations and guidelines for designing software will improve the accessibility of distance learning software for these user groups.

The purpose of the industry study was to document universal design practices within industries represented by the six product lines selected for study. Five categories of facilitators and barriers related to accessible design were examined: design process related, organizational, informational, financial, and legal.

Results from the industry study found that the most common approaches to addressing accessibility issues were: increasing awareness of employees, integrating accessibility requirements into the design process, performing accessibility verification testing, and establishing an accessibility program office.

NCD's study results and analyses demonstrate that the classes of people making up the market for accessible products and services include the following users:

- Users with permanent disabilities
- Users with temporary disabilities
- Users with functional limitations due to situational factors
- Users with low literacy skills
- Users in low bandwidth areas
- Users desiring increased functionality and usability
- Users who do not speak English as their primary language

• Users in high-population-density areas
• Users who are elderly

From this research, we learned that designing with access in mind can significantly increase the size of ICT markets on a global basis. Good business practices dictate that designers and engineers avoid excluding large groups of consumers from accessing and using ICT. We determined that the groups at the highest risk of unintentional exclusion are:

• Persons with disabilities
• Individuals 65+ years old
• Consumers living within low-bandwidth information infrastructures
• Users of English as a Second Language (ESL)
• Tourists traveling to non-native language destinations
• Consumers living in high-density populations

The fiscal or business implications are clear: consumers spend one out of every four ICT dollars worldwide, and ICT spending per capita has increased every year since 2001 (Digital Planet 2006). For example, ICT spending per capita increased from $538 to $567 between 2005 and 2006. Taking into consideration that there are an estimated 600 million persons living with disabilities worldwide and that consumers spend one out of every four ICT dollars worldwide, the market base of consumers with disabilities is a significant one.

Persons with disabilities told us that when it comes to ICT, they want to use the same products that everyone else uses and, in doing so, they do not want to be limited to specialized products that are more costly.

From our *Design for Inclusion* research study, we learned that implementation of universal design is the best way to satisfy this desire of persons with disabilities, while also providing more cost-effective products for all users. Furthermore, we concluded that products and services that come closer to accommodating a variety of physical and cognitive differences will benefit users and companies alike.

Success Stories: Harnessing the Power of Accessible and Assistive Information and Communications Technologies

This chapter focuses on particularly noteworthy success stories regarding the role of assistive information and communication technologies in major sectors of society, such as education, employment, and business. It includes several employment-related stories, which examine, among other topics, the benefits of using assistive ICTs to create a digital office from home, one company's ability to adapt to the needs of its employees with disabilities, and several initiatives established to provide specialized vocational training to persons with disabilities using assistive ICTs in the developing world. Likewise, this chapter will expose a number of educational initiatives aimed at increasing students' potential both in and outside of the classroom, focusing in large part on the role of ICT applications in fostering self-expression. We conclude the chapter by presenting a case of a local public-private partnership that was formed to help make a specialized assistive technology solution affordable.

Telework: Opening New Employment Opportunities for Persons with Disabilities

By Ilene Morris-Sambur
Founder and CEO, Coraworks

If we stop long enough to reflect on life's lessons, some of us are blessed with the ability to use our expertise to give back to others. I would like to share the discovery of what I feel is my purpose and my life's passion – a mission that has led me to what I and many others believe are solutions for dramatically increasing employment opportunities for individuals with disabilities.

The past 25 years of my career as a "turnaround consultant" for financially distressed companies led me to the creation of CORA, Creating Opportunities by Recognizing Abilities. Serving as both interim CEO and CFO of financially distressed companies, I have trained over a thousand managers and staff to improve profits and productivity in over 35 industries. Always in search of the ideal employee for my clients, I often wondered what happened to the old work ethic where an employee was competent, loyal, productive, and enthusiastic about the success of the business. The employee should be eager to learn and assume more responsibility, as well as be excited about his or her company's future and the role he or she can play in helping to achieve those objectives.

Through a series of synchronistic events, I was able to look at my life experiences and come to the realization that there is a very competent underemployed population that, once given the opportunity to work from home, would excel at telework. There are many extremely talented individuals with disabilities, who are not able to work outside of their homes. Millions of individuals with disabilities are unemployed, and CORA clearly demonstrates that these workers are more dedicated, focused, productive, and serious about their work performance than the average employee. Given the necessary tools to help apply their skills in a remote worker realm, and a strong mentoring and support system, they excel at telework.

Telework is an ideal solution that results in many benefits for a diverse range of individuals, including those with disabilities, elderly persons, 24/7 caregivers, and military spouses. With a very strong involvement in the future of the "outsourced world," as well as communication opportunities for individuals with disabilities, CORA aims to educate as many companies as possible to identify telework opportunities that will help to increase the company's profits and productivity. In essence, we provide supervised telework training, placement, and mentoring services for individuals with disabilities to work from their homes. We are serving individuals whose special needs make it such that they have no other choice but to work from their homes. The benefits of telework were officially recognized in 2006 by the Secretary of Labor, Elaine Chao, when she awarded CORA with the New Freedom Initiative Award, which was presented to one non-profit corporation and one individual for creating innovative work solutions for individuals with disabilities.

Among our various activities, CORA provides telework pilot programs to various military hospitals such as at the Walter Reed Army Hospital. We have found that, if during rehabilitation, veterans with disabilities engage in a meaningful activity that allows them to be productive, they are much more inclined to continue such activities in the long-term once they return home. This rehabilitative technique has proven extremely successful in helping veterans with disabilities accelerate their recovery time by providing a vehicle through which they can focus on their abilities and away from their disabilities.

I was very fortunate to have met the CEO and President, Chuck Wilsker, of an organization called TELCOA, the Telework Coalition. Chuck and I both feel very strongly that work is something one does – not a place one goes. Likewise, we see the future as bringing work to the people, not the people to work; and with assistive technology, such lifestyles can easily be made available to individuals with a broad range of disabilities.

The Telework Coalition, TelCoa, is a non-profit association headquartered in Washington, DC that was founded six years ago by individuals with many years of experience addressing issues relating to telework and telecommuting. TelCoa's mission and goals are to enable and support virtual, mobile, and distributed work through research, education, technology, and legislation. TelCoa acquires information through many means, disseminates it to interested individuals and groups, reviews and assesses technologies that facilitate the implementation or expansion of telework programs (e.g. broadband Internet access, secure remote access solutions, video collaboration, personal communication devices, etc.), and works with federal, state, and local legislators to encourage legislation favorable to telework. By working in conjunction with TelCoa, CORA is able to stay on the forefront of developments in the telework industry and thus better respond to the needs of those it aims to serve.

Most people who begin Telework through CORA stay with the program for a very long time. Such long-term commitment is due, in part, to the mentoring services that we offer. If a CORA employee is having trouble, he or she can consult with a mentor via instant messaging at anytime during the work day. We also provide mental health counselors who are available around the clock. A number of our workers live in rural communities where job opportunities and support is limited, making our support system a major factor contributing to their ability to succeed at telework. This same model could be instituted anywhere in the world where hi-speed internet is available.

In order to give the reader a better idea of the kind of impact Telework can have, I would like to draw attention to the example of Todd Arnold, a vocational rehabilitation referral from Stout University. Todd has worked with CORA for almost a year now. Todd has never heard my voice, and we communicate through instant messaging only. I have never met a young man as personable, bright, and with as great an attitude as Todd. There are different types of telework that Todd can do and does do. The following is a brief, albeit very telling interview, conducted via instant message with Todd at G3ict Global Forum this past March:

> *Todd Arnold:* Good morning Ilene and everybody in attendance there in New York, I appreciate the opportunity to tell my story and help others in this situation.

> *Ilene Morris-Sambur:* Todd, how has the Internet changed your life?

Todd Arnold: I can now play games, listen to music, watch TV and videos, buy and sell items on E-bay, follow my favorite sports games, use MySpace, play fantasy football and baseball, watch DVDs, email, be in real time contact with relatives, friends, and co-workers, engage in on-line education, have access to employment opportunities, read my local newspaper online, conduct information research, and participate in on-line surveys.

Ilene Morris-Sambur: Todd, can you tell us about your life – where you are from etc.?

Todd Arnold: My name is Todd Arnold, and I live in Black Creek, Wisconsin. I have a muscle disease called Spinal Muscular Atrophy. I am totally bed-ridden. I have no movement in my arms, and most of the things I need to do have to be done by other people.

Ilene Morris-Sambur: Please describe some of the programs that you have been currently using?

Todd Arnold: The technology that I am using right now is the Dell Inspiron 8200 Laptop Computer with wireless broadband internet access.

Ilene Morris-Sambur: Could you please tell us some more about the kind of work that you do? What is your job, your position, your responsibilities? In particular, how has the internet helped you and changed your life? By the way, Todd is communicating by speaking very softly into a microphone, which is enough input for the computer to transmit messages to us; however, if we would try to hear it through this computer or through a phone it would probably be a bit too soft for us to hear. Despite the fact that he is ventilator-dependent and completely bedridden, he usually does not stop talking!

Todd Arnold: I do website building, medical billing and, for CORA, I have been working on database data entry and some accounting. Without the Internet and the technology I use, working from my home would be impossible – not to mention a number of others things I use the Internet for in my personal life. I have a whole new life. I feel my life has purpose again. I keep in touch with my friends and family, which was difficult to do before the Internet. My best friend from high school, for instance, lives in California, and his little girl calls me Uncle Todd when she sees me on my webcam. It is truly a blessing for me.

Ilene Morris-Sambur: Thank you very much, Todd, for your time and for showing us how you feel about being able to successfully work from home.

I felt that it was important to share Todd's perspective on outsourced work to spread awareness about the profound impact such flexibility can have on both the employee and the employer. With companies trying to cut costs and find ways to increase revenue, outsourcing is becoming more commonplace in the workforce. More and more companies are outsourcing jobs that can be done via telework. Accounting, data entry, customer service, collections, web design, and research, to name but a few, can all be done by persons with disabilities from the home thanks to the advances of technology and the Internet. To help further this goal, CORA has formed Business Partner Alliances with companies that understand the significance and benefits of working together to help maximize telework opportunities for individuals with disabilities. Walgreens, Raytheon, Pride Industries, and AARP are only a few of the many companies and organizations that understand the significance of supporting our mission by helping us to prove – CORAworks!

Assistive technologies, such as voice recognition software, adaptive keyboards, electronic pointing devices, sit-and-touch systems, wands, and sticks, to name a few, have proven extremely useful for persons with disabilities in their professional, as well as personal lives. Moreover, necessary vocational training can easily be carried out by means of the Internet, e-mail, or instant messaging programs – and even via computer-to-computer online calling. The Internet in and of itself has the ability to counteract professional and social exclusion and guarantee a much better quality of life by bringing the outside world to workers at home, continuing their career advancement, and enabling them to constantly interact with co-workers, friends, and family members. Technological solutions make it possible to introduce a better quality of life for persons who are otherwise often cut off from much of the world.

POETA: Fighting Exclusion in the Americas with Assistive and Accessible Technologies

By René Léon
Program Coordinator, POETA, Organization of American States

There are approximately 80 million persons with disabilities in Latin America, ninety percent of which are unemployed and essentially excluded from the workforce. Most of them live in abject poverty and do not have access to formal and/or informal education. Thus, it is our responsibility to provide persons with disabilities with the necessary skills and opportunities to apply for and hold a job, earn a living, and become independent.

Established with support from the Microsoft Corporation in 2004, the Partnership in Opportunities for Employment through Technology in the Americas (POETA) is a hemispheric initiative between the Organization of American States (OAS) and its affiliate, The Trust for the Americas, to fight poverty and improve competitiveness in Latin America though technology and job-readiness training in marginalized communities.

POETA has three main components: (i) a technology center, opened in partnership with a local university, NGO, and/or a government agency with experience working with persons with disabilities and possessing the necessary infrastructure to operate/manage the center, (ii) a job-readiness module that helps the program's beneficiaries, among other things, to better prepare for an interview and obtain a job, and (iii) a public awareness campaign, which helps the Trust to promote the program's goals in the public and private sectors, as well as in the community.

Each POETA center adapts to the specific needs of the underserved population at hand. With the knowledge and experience of local partner organizations, the Trust has been able to establish POETA centers where there is the greatest need. To this end, POETA serves as a model for public-private sector cooperation, with more than 100 public and private sector partners leveraging knowledge, goodwill, resources, and infrastructure across a dozen countries.

POETA benefits approximately 12,500 people directly each year. Participants usually range in age from 18 to 30, most of them with disabilities. To date, The Trust for the Americas has thirty-nine operational POETA centers in the following Latin American countries: Argentina, Colombia, Dominican Republic, Ecuador, El Salvador, Guatemala, Honduras, Mexico, Panama, Peru, and Venezuela.

The Trust equips each POETA center with adaptive technology that enables persons with disabilities to use and take full advantage of the computers made available to them. The adaptive technology available at the POETA centers includes, but is not limited to:

- Trackballs: a bigger version of the standard mouse. Some do not consider the Trackball to be an adaptive technology because it can be used by persons with or without disabilities. However, this device allows the user to maximize his activity on the computer – especially in conjunction with hand wands and mouth sticks. People who have tremors in their hands, for instance, can manipulate the Trackball with their feet.

- Dragon Naturally Speaking, a voice recognition software that allows the user to dictate quickly and accurately into almost any Windows-based application.

- IntelliKeys: an alternative keyboard that can attach to any computer and enable students with physical, visual, or cognitive disabilities to easily type, navigate screen displays, and execute many other common commands.

- JAWS (Job Access with Speech): a screen reader whose purpose is to maximize Windows accessibility for blind or visually impaired users.

The POETA program is an example of how technology can change the lives of and empower those who are underserved by today's society. This Microsoft-sponsored initiative is enabling persons with disabilities in Latin America to better their lives and those of their families. Yet, although POETA provides persons with disabilities with an opportunity to become better prepared citizens and pursue fulfilling careers, there is still much more to be done. Many persons with disabilities remain illiterate and unemployed. As such, it is POETA's hope that the public and private sectors will continue to work together not only to enhance the quality of local workforces throughout the hemisphere, but also to enable more persons with disabilities to lead healthy and productive lives. Without such strategic partnership, the achievement of mainstream social and economic inclusion of persons with disabilities is not possible.

Making Accessibility Work for All in Education

By Steven M. Rothstein
President, Perkins School for the Blind

Perkins School for the Blind is the first school for the blind in the United States. Within a few short years of its founding in 1829, Perkins became known for its effective instructional techniques, including teaching Laura Bridgman, the first known deaf-blind person to be educated. Later, a much more famous student and her teacher – Helen Keller and Anne Sullivan – came to Perkins on their way to breaking down barriers and perceptions about what people who are blind or deaf-blind could accomplish. Perkins has been and continues to be a source of inspiration and opportunity for people who are blind, deaf-blind, or blind with multiple disabilities. Throughout the past 178 years, we have explored the use of appropriate technology.

Today, Perkins is a world-renowned center of excellence in the field of blindness and deaf-blindness education. Perkins' programs and services benefit more than 87,000 individuals worldwide. The fundamental mission of Perkins School for the Blind is to help children and adults who are blind, deaf-blind, and blind with multiple disabilities to reach their greatest possible independence. Through the development of knowledge, skills, and confidence, students learn to live, work, and function as independently as possible within their communities. Teacher preparation is also an important part of our mission. Since 1920, Perkins has trained teachers from both the U.S.

and around the world and has helped universities develop or expand teacher training programs.

From the beginning, Perkins School for the Blind has identified solutions to problems and issues faced by people who are blind and deaf-blind. Technology has often been a keystone of these solutions. One such undertaking was the development of embossed type – a precursor to Braille – to facilitate reading by the blind and deaf-blind. Since 1951, Perkins has manufactured and sold more than 300,000 Perkins Braillers®, the standard for brailling excellence, in 170 countries. Today, the power of technology is providing a wide variety of assistive devices that aid in teaching and learning, as well as in independent living for students and adults who are blind and deaf-blind. Both on the Perkins School for the Blind's campus and in our work around the world, our goal is to provide empowering technological resources that are appropriate for each individual.

In 1989, with the generous support of the Conrad N. Hilton Foundation, Perkins formally established a comprehensive program to support the education of children who are deaf-blind and blind with multiple disabilities throughout the world. The primary focus of our international efforts is on building capacity at all levels of society for independent, sustainable educational services. When this program was initiated, fewer then 250 children who were deaf-blind or blind with multiple disabilities were being educated in specialized programs in the developing world. With the help of Perkins, today, our local partners provide direct services to more than 8,000 children in developing countries each year. In addition, approximately 200,000 children, family members, teachers, and professionals have directly benefited from the Program's activities, which include our teacher training programs, the help we provide in developing curricula and vocational training programs, and our work to ensure that governments recognize the specialized educational and health needs of this marginalized population.

Advocacy is another important part of our international mission. Over the last two decades, Perkins has worked with government officials in more than 20 countries to improve education, health, and disability policies. For instance, through our annual training program for the Ministry of Education in Kenya, we have raised awareness about the needs of children with multiple disabilities. This greater awareness has led to changes in policies that benefit children who are deaf-blind or with multiple disabilities. Due to the efforts of Perkins and its local partners, the government of Brazil now recognizes deaf-blindness as a unique disability. These are just a few examples of the impact of Perkins International's work in the policy arena.

Despite the tireless efforts of Perkins School for the Blind and other organizations and agencies, the need for educational programs for children who are blind, deaf-blind, and blind with multiple disabilities remains great. There are currently six million children who are blind or visually impaired around the world. Less than 10 percent of these children in developing countries have access to education.

The work of Perkins School for the Blind is guided by many of the same principles of Education for All Children with Visual Impairment, a global campaign to address key Millennium Development Goals. Those principles state that:

- Every child can learn

- No child should be denied the opportunity to achieve his or her potential
- Solutions lie within each society
- Parents and family members play a key role as advocates and teachers

The use of new appropriate technologies continues to play an important role in achieving this vision. As sighted persons have access to a range of technology – from personal computers to hand-held devices – so too should persons who are visually impaired – with or without disabilities. Both low and high technology devices provide more opportunities to learn and greater independence for people who are visually impaired.

One example of a valuable low technology option is the Perkins Brailler®. It is the most reliable pathway to literacy for persons who are blind or visually impaired. Access to the Perkins Brailler® enables children and adults to both read and write Braille, entering the workforce fully literate and independent. For instance, 90 percent of blind persons who know Braille are employed, yet over 70 percent without Braille skills are not. The Perkins Brailler contributes in yet another way to the independence of persons with disabilities in developing countries, and that is through the assembling and repairing of Braillers, which can be a source of livelihood for many people. It is critical that literacy be accessible to all, including those for whom Braille writing machines are not appropriate. Assistive technologies, such as talking books and audio-recorded subtitles, also play an important role in the promotion of literacy for persons who are blind or visually impaired.

Since the 1970s, when Raymond Kurzweil invented the first print-to-speech reading machine, high technology solutions have been opening new doors for communication, employment, learning, mobility, leisure, and social activities. In the educational context, technology is a vital tool for teaching and learning. Inclusive technology for persons who are blind or visually impaired – from screen readers to enable individuals who are blind to use a computer to personal digital assistants for daily living and workplace use – are developed and improved every day. Several main examples of such assistive technology solutions are:

- Personal digital assistants designed specifically for the blind that enable students to take notes in Braille, access the Internet, and use tools such as calculators and calendars
- Braille and assistive hardware, including Braille embossers and talking tactile tablets, which can transform the ways in which persons who are visually impaired access graphical information
- Personal talking book players that make literacy possible for children and adults who are visually impaired
- Electronic video magnification devices that magnify text and images on a computer for people with low vision
- Educational assistive software that allows children and adults who are blind to use computers independently

The new Convention on the Rights of Persons with Disabilities will have an important impact on the lives of people in every country. The implementation of inclusive information and communication technologies is a key element of the Convention. Helen Keller communicated with her teacher, her family members, and others in different ways – including Braille and hand-on-hand sign language. Perkins is committed to ensuring that persons who are blind or visually impaired continue to benefit from all forms of communication, including those made possible by new technologies.

Assisting Self-Expression with Technology: the Yonsei Rehabilitation School Experience

By Dr. Sukja Park
Principal, Yonsei Rehabilitation School,
Synthesis of presentation from G3ict-KADO Meeting in Seoul, Korea

I am SukJa Park, the principal of the Yonsei Rehabilitation School. Our school was established for the first time as a private school for young persons with disabilities in Korea, educating a student body where 80% of our students could not communicate with words. I started to work with this school in 1975 and immediately began garnering support from related medical experts to help persons with disabilities to express their views. In this context, the work of the Korea Agency for Digital Opportunity and Promotion (KADO) and that of the Global Initiative for Inclusive Information and Communication Technologies (G3ict) is very much in line with the objectives of the school.

Although persons with disabilities can utilize ICT technologies in a myriad of ways, we at the Yonsei Rehabilitation School believe that the expression of ideas is the first and foremost important use. Using ICT-related tools, we have even been able to help children with the most severe disabilities express their views.

In 1976, I began disability-related studies at university and then later went on to earn a Ph.D. in Disability Education. When I joined the Yonsei Rehabilitation School, I immediately began experimenting with ways to encourage students to express their views and consequently embark on a unique process of "self-discovery." In collaboration with the language therapist at Severance Hospital, we aimed to support as much as possible technological solutions for persons with disabilities.

Those who are unable to speak are equal human beings on this earth, and should be viewed as possessing an equally valuable human dignity. At the Yonsei Rehabilitation School, we strongly believe in helping our students to cultivate their own views and opinions by letting them express themselves through the use of information and communications technologies. I received a doctorate degree after eight years of study, and the subject of my thesis was Spatial Education for those who are mute. Since 80%-90% of our school's students cannot speak, it was pertinent that I create a way for them to express themselves.

By using voice-out devices, I believed that we could help our students to express their views. Those who cannot use their own voice use voice-assistive technologies, allowing them to improve their capability to express their ideas and views. In addition, by using these assistive technology devices, we actually succeeded in reducing certain problematic behaviors in some of our students, as well as improving motor skills in others. It is important to mention that there are not many students at our special school whose IQ is above 100. In fact, only one or two percent might have an IQ above 100, and many of them will never be able to learn to speak. Because of a lack of voice development due to brain impairment or a malfunction in the brain structure, such children usually use body language, facial expressions, pictures, laughing, crying, screaming, or basic hand language to communicate.

Our teachers try to devise curriculums suitable for children with disabilities, but consistently struggle to help students who cannot speak to express themselves. In these cases, alternative techniques or technologies must be employed. For example, if a child with a disability wants to say to his or her mother: "I don't want to eat meat today", he can express such an opinion by using an assistive communication device. This solution will help the child to have better communication with his family members, friends, and teachers. On the other hand, if the child can speak, she can use the assistive communication device to adapt herself to the community environment around her, improving overall social adaptability. I like to send students to the store to help them experience what its like to function in a real world situation. I have them ask change after purchasing an item or interact with the workers by expressing their views using their high-tech devices.

Now, some might say: "Why don't you just use body language, crying, or laughing to help the children exchange their views and opinions?"; and some parents are worried that, if there is too much focus on using assistive technologies, the student with a disability might never speak. At times, we are able to make a judgment based on a facial expression; however, certain children have disabilities that prevent them from expressing emotion entirely. Some students cannot even produce the appropriate sounds from their mouths or make basic signs with their hands. Non-verbal language thus needs to be developed through the use of assistive technology.

Before the widespread use of assistive technologies, we relied mostly on the use of pictographs. In 1980, when pictographs were not widely used throughout the world, a hospital located in Ontario, Canada actually developed pictograph symbols to facilitate communication with patients with disabilities. The Canadian hospital began developing alternative communicative strategies, around which there were many forums and discussions, at a relatively early point in time. The Yonsei Rehabilitation Hospital, being the largest medical center for persons with disabilities in Korea, attempted to follow the lead of this Canadian hospital. Many of the signs that originated in Canada, being mostly composed of line drawings and basic symbols, quickly spread throughout the world. Pictograph symbols, such as those for "house", "book", "car", "animal", "ear", and "eye", as well as those for plus and minus symbols, were widely used for communication – especially in Europe and its surrounding regions. When it came to complex symbols, the trend was to combine several symbols into one, such as the first pictograph below for "house."

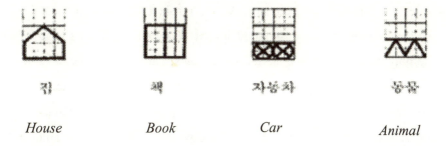

House　　　　　Book　　　　　Car　　　　　Animal

In the 1990s, the teachers at our rehabilitation school visited a number of European countries that had already adapted this pictograph system. In the 1980s in Korea, this kind of non-verbal system of symbols had not yet been employed, but has since become widely adapted across the country. The target group for this pictograph system includes cerebral-palsy and autistic students, as well as those with mental disorders or head injuries resulting in the loss of speech. Those who use assistive technology devices in conjunction with this symbol system use a picture board, letter board, communication board, or IT technology-based voice output device.

What is the reason for this effort? First, it aims at developing speaking capabilities and also provides social interaction. We have a lot of devices at our school, and we are able to record the tablet material onto our PCs in order to enable the students to also use the computer. These computer programs, in turn, help children express their views in an efficient way.

One case that I think is worth mentioning is the case of a spitting student that we once had in our school. When I came close to the student, he would often spit on me. I had trouble understanding why he often displayed such behavior. When I asked that question to the student's mother, she responded that it was just the child's way of getting attention. So, we started to pay closer attention to the student, and taught him that spitting was not a good behavior. Rather than spitting, we showed him how to use the assistive technology device to express certain opinions. Our approach worked, and we were able to achieve successful behavior modification. We since received news that this former student has been employed by an American company!

I have conducted a number of experiments on the problems that can result from students who do not speak. If we let the students know that certain behaviors are unacceptable, then they usually want to correct such behavior. However, if they have no other alternative to self-expression, they have no choice but to repeat the behavior that we deem "bad." I have found that, if students have access to assistive technology devices, they are eager to use such devices to express themselves. Sometimes we organize what we call "oral play activities," whereby volunteers take a student role and students assume a teacher role.

Students tend to respond to such role-playing activities, which allow them to experiment with familiar day-to-day communicative interactions through the use of their assistive technology devices.

Our goal at the Yonsei Rehabilitation School is to provide pleasure and satisfaction to our students, as well as to give way to their hopes and dreams. In order to achieve this goal, we much prioritize programs that provide access to assistive ICTs.

Accessible Education for People with Special Needs as the Basis for Creating an Open Information Society

By Dr. Boris Kotsik, Director and
Dr. Natalia Tokareva, Project Manager
UNESCO Institute for Information Technologies in Education
(UNESCO IITE)

Aiming at reinforcing the potential of UNESCO Member States in information and communication technology (ICT) applications for the development of education, UNESCO IITE concentrates its efforts on training and retraining activities in the use of ICTs for educators. Key trends in training educators and, accordingly, main directions in the development of instruction materials are determined on the basis of close cooperation with international organizations and leading experts on ICT application in education.

One of the most important directions of IITE activities is improving quality and access to education for persons with disabilities by means of ICTs. The mission of the project is to provide increasing access to knowledge and information for all, in order to facilitate active participation in civil society – including in scientific, economic, social, political, and cultural activities. The main objective of the UNESCO IITE project entitled "Information and Communication Technologies in Education of People with Special Needs" is to reinforce national capacities in education and social inclusion of people with special needs by using a systemic application of ICTs. The project targets the training of policy developers and decision makers, managers, administrators, specialists in teacher training and retraining institutions, specialists of social care agencies, educators, and instruction support specialists engaged in education and social rehabilitation of people with special needs.

Since the beginning of the project in 1999, the Institute held a number of international expert meetings and workshops in partnership with well-known experts from 13 countries, including the United Kingdom, Italy, the Netherlands, Japan, Australia, and the United States. Recommendations of international experts provided the basis for development of information materials and of the analytical survey "Information and Communication Technologies in Special Education" (2001), which show the current state, prospects, and main trends of ICT application in special needs education. Accumulated experience also enabled IITE to develop the specialized training course "ICTs in Education for People with Special Needs" (2006). The course was developed by a team of international specialists from Italy, the Russian Federation, Australia, Denmark, Iceland, and Spain and was headed by Dr. Edwards from the United Kingdom. The course offers the opportunity for a wide range of specialists, involved in education of people with special needs, to acquire knowledge and develop practical skills on organizational, pedagogical, psychological, and technological aspects of ICT application in face-to-face and distance education of students with disabilities. Course materials represent the best international experience in the field of general and specific ICT applications in education for persons with physical, visual, hearing, speech and language, cognitive, and learning impairments. Particular emphasis of the course is placed on the basic aspects of ICT policy development in special needs education (SNE), including promotion of

ICT infrastructure, integration of ICTs into curriculum, and training and retraining of ICT specialists in special education.

The training course consists of four modules. Module 1, "Special Needs Education in the Information Age," explains the changing role of education and the necessity of ICT implementation into SNE. The module presents the issue of equal opportunity in education and relates it to the need for equal access to information for each and every member of a society, especially for persons with special needs. Particular emphasis is placed on the social drive toward inclusion in education and on main SNE organization principles. Module 2, "Assistive Technologies for Students with SNE," provides explanations of assistive technologies, their classifications, and descriptions of application areas. To this extent, Module 2 addresses the use of assistive technologies for educational purposes in relation to the needs of six main groups of impairments: physical, visual, hearing, speech and language, cognitive, and learning. Module 3, "Distance Technologies for Students with SNE," presents an overview of the evolution and main features of ICT-based distance learning and teaching methods. It focuses on accessibility barriers to educational resources for students with disabilities and provides descriptions of ways to overcome them. Module 4, "ICT Policy in Special Needs Education," provides an ample overview of the key activities of ICT policy development and implementation in SNE, including the promotion of ICT infrastructures for SNE, integration of ICTs into SNE curriculums, and training and retraining of ICT specialists in SNE.

The training materials of the course have been translated into the Russian language and adapted to fit the specific conditions of the Russian educational system.

The main achievements of the project thus far include an elaboration and publication of the analytical survey "Information and Communication Technology in Special Education" (2001), elaboration and publication of the specialized training course and syllabus "ICTs in Education for People with Special Needs" (2006), and the organization of two international expert meetings, four international workshops, and five training sessions. Over 200 specialists from 11 countries were trained in these training sessions. Furthermore, a specialized training course was successfully presented at six international conferences and attracted much interest among attending specialists (France, 2005; Indonesia, 2005; Russian Federation, 2005, 2007; Latvia, 2006, Tunisia, 2007).

In 2007, IITE started to elaborate on recommendations for promoting suitable digital environments for education and lifelong learning of persons with disabilities, including the development of standards and guidelines for the use of ICT in education and for the training of educational and IT personnel on e-Accessibility of educational resources.

UNESCO IITE continues to disseminate teaching and learning practices in the context of special educational environments through a set of ever-evolving training sessions and workshops for different groups of specialists working in education for persons with SEN. Following the effort to reinforce national potential of UNESCO Member States, IITE plans to maintain dedicated research endeavors and develop new recommendations and guidelines for establishing appropriate conditions for equal access to education for all – even for those who are restricted in their ability to acquire or perceive information.

For more information concerning IITE training activities, one may visit the IITE website at http://www.iite.ru

Leveling the Playing Field and Changing What It Means to Be Blind

By Larry Campbell
Administrator, Overbrook International Program
Tamas Babinszki, Overbrook International Program Alumnus

Not since the creation of the Braille writing system in 1829 has any single development had such a profound impact on the lives of blind individuals as those created by developments in assistive technology. These new technologies made possible by the digital age have truly leveled the playing field by giving individuals with a disabling visual impairment real-time access to information. Lack of real-time access to information has until recent decades placed persons with a visual impairment at a distinct disadvantage. True, many have found ways to excel in spite of these barriers, but often at high personal cost.

The Beginnings

Recognizing the profound impact that these new developments in technology were likely to have on the education and employment prospects of blind individuals throughout the world, the Overbrook School for Blind developed the Overbrook International Program in 1985. This program provided a cross-cultural experience and a year of intensive study in computer technology, English as a Second Language (ESL), and leadership development to a select group of blind students between 16-21 years of age. Over the course of the next thirteen years, three-hundred-and-four blind students from forty-four countries representing all regions of the world came to Philadelphia to live and learn alongside fellow blind students.

Most of the individuals who participated in this program refer to it as a "life-changing experience." Not only were they away from home for the first time and learning to cope with a totally new environment, food, and language, but they were introduced to the powers of assistive technology and pushed to expand themselves, educationally, socially, and culturally. Many of these young people had never used – or perhaps even seen – a computer before arriving in Philadelphia. However, as anyone who has been around a blind individual for any length of time knows, assistive technology enables blind persons to access the world through information in a way that makes it difficult to ever separate them from their newfound "tools of liberation." In short, these young people quickly discovered that assistive technology gave them freedom and access to a world of information that they never imagined possible.

Achieving and Sharing

On an early winter day in 1995, we received a call from the Ukrainian Embassy in Washington. A member of the Ukranian Parliament was visiting the United States and had learned about a blind Ukranian student studying at Overbrook. He asked the embassy to make arrangements for him to visit. We felt there was no better way of introducing him to the program than to allow Victor, the Ukranian student he had learned about, to do so. About an hour after his tour began, I walked into one of the computer classrooms where Victor was enthusiastically introducing the visitor to the wonders of the Jaws screenreader program. The parliamentarian was completely captivated by the "talking computer" and the lesson he was receiving from Victor, who only a few months earlier had "met" his first computer.

Six months later, Victor was back in Ukraine determined to share his knowledge with fellow blind students. Soon, he attracted the attention of several international donor organizations, and the computer center for the blind in Lviv was opened. However, Victor did not stop there. He returned to the United States and earned a degree in computer science and has since served as a trainer for Overbrook's international outreach program on a number of occasions – first in Thailand and then in the Philippines, Cambodia, and Vietnam. He enthusiastically shared his knowledge with many young blind individuals in Southeast Asia who had not had the benefit of spending a year at the Overbrook International Program. Today, some twelve years after "meeting" his first computer in that classroom at Overbrook, his mastery of technology, his willingness and ability to share that knowledge with others, and his exceptional work ethic have led to his current position as Director of Accessibility for the Yahoo Corporation. Victor's story is typical of the way in which technology is transforming lives and changing what it means to be blind.

In the early 1990's, as Overbrook followed up with the graduates of the International Program, it became clear to us that, while the program was having a profound impact on the lives of that select group of students who were privileged enough to attend the program, we were only "scratching the surface" of the need that existed in most countries where the use of technology as a powerful tool was for the first time being understood. We grappled with the question of how we might more effectively reach larger numbers of blind children and adults, and from these discussions, Overbrook's International Outreach Program emerged.

While the management of Overbrook was enthusiastic about this new phase of the program, that enthusiasm was not universally shared by many of our colleagues outside of the school. Some in the field of development quite frankly thought we had lost our minds. They reasoned that, while these technologies were appropriate for the industrialized West, they were a waste of time and resources for developing countries. We felt otherwise.

Fortunately for Overbrook, so did individuals like George Soros and his Open Society Institute, as well as The Nippon Foundation – both of whom took a longer term view of these developments and shared our vision.

Admittedly, these technologies were costly and out of reach for most blind individuals. However, such had been the case with earlier technologies. For instance, remember those huge and expensive early "pocket calculators" or those pricey, yet miraculous, fax machines? We knew that the costs of those products would eventually go down and calculated that these reductions, combined with anticipated increases in GDP for many countries, would make previously unaffordable products affordable. In the meantime, even if not widely accessible by the average individual, there were still ways that these technologies could save money – even in poor countries.

The Network Concept

Aside from the need expressed by our international graduates and by those who had funded their participation in our Philadelphia-based program, my personal experience of working in these countries and meeting with those who had begun to explore these technologies convinced me of the potential value of "technology networks."

The fundamental idea behind these networks was to accelerate the use of assistive technologies for the blind by providing the opportunity for individuals and organizations to come together to establish priorities, share information, improve the skills and knowledge of a core group of "master trainers", develop training and public education materials, and support innovative initiatives that would expand access to assistive technologies at both national and regional levels. Within the context of developing and emerging market economies, such a work plan seemed particularly important as developments across the field of assistive technology were evolving at such a rapid pace that it was virtually impossible for all but the wealthiest countries to keep up.

Networks in Action

In 1996, the Overbrook Board approved the first of our regional outreach programs: a program that initially served Hungary, Poland, Lithuania, and the Czech and Slovak Republics and later Romania, Latvia, and Estonia. As the countries of the former "Eastern Bloc" struggled with the transition to a market economy, persons with disabilities found themselves in a very difficult situation. The centrally planned "industries" that had for decades provided sheltered employment to persons with disabilities were crumbling under the weight of market reform. Blind and other persons with disabilities needed new skill sets and new tools to compete in the emerging market economy. Many blind individuals saw technology as a kind of "silver lining" during these dark days of transition. There was tremendous motivation on the part of organizations of the blind, and particularly amongst the younger generations of blind persons, to turn this difficult situation into new opportunity. This motivation, combined with the high standards in math and science that were typical of the educational systems of these countries, made Eastern Europe an excellent testing ground for this concept of regional networks. With support from both the Overbrook Board of Managers and George Soros' Open Society Institute, the EASTERN EUROPEAN NETWORK ON ACCESS TECHNOLOGY – EENAT – was born.

Over the next several years, EENAT was able to bring together a number of our International Program graduates, along with blind leaders and educators, to form a regional network that significantly expanded the skills of teachers, localized popular software applications, developed local language training and public education materials, and supported innovative programs that demonstrated how assistive technology could be used in an appropriate and cost-effective manner to increase access to education and new open-market employment opportunities for blind individuals.

As EENAT was evolving, a number of countries in Southeast Asia turned to Overbrook for assistance. The first regional conference on assistive technology for the blind, organized by the Malaysian Association for the Blind in November, 1993, ended with a very specific resolution calling on Overbrook to extend the reach of its international program through bases within Southeast Asia. Over the next few years, Overbrook carried out extensive consultation with governments and organizations of the blind, along with education and rehabilitation centers serving blind persons.

These consultations eventually led to discussions with The Nippon Foundation that had for several years provided scholarship support for a number of blind students attending the International Program in Philadelphia. The concept of developing a regional network to expand access to new technologies for blind persons in Southeast Asia appealed to the foundation. As a result, a permanent endowment fund was established at Overbrook to support these networks, and the OVERBROOK-NIPPON NETWORK ON EDUCATIONAL TECHOLOGY – ON-NET – was officially establish in mid-1998.

ON-NET currently serves eight countries in Southeast Asia: Cambodia, Indonesia, Laos, Malaysia, Myanmar, Philippines, Thailand, and Vietnam. Initially, this regional program focused on using new developments in technology to help increase Braille textbook production and training for instructors from throughout the region at its base at Mahidol University in Thailand. Over the past nine years, the results of working together have been nothing short of remarkable. There has been a dramatic increase in access to assistive technologies at schools and in the workplace and significantly larger numbers of blind students are pursuing higher education, taking on new jobs, and, by their positive example, changing public attitudes.

Today, ON-NET and its local partners have significantly expanded access to technology, as well as the ways in which technology can improve the quality of life of blind children and adults in the region. While space does not permit me to go into detail here, I would like to illustrate with a few concrete examples of how ON-NET partners are effectively using new developments in assistive technology to change what it means to be blind.

Indonesia

Development of online Braille libraries is allowing Braille producers to co-operate in the production of Braille-ready files that are posted on a central Internet site in Jakarta. The files can then be downloaded and embossed by individuals, schools, and other organizations throughout the country. The online database saves the Indonesian government a lot of money by preventing needless duplication efforts and by eliminating transportation costs that are associated with the shipment of Braille books in a country that stretches over a huge area consisting of more than 7,000 islands.

Cambodia

In a country where education of blind children only began in 1992, the development of a Khmer language Braille translation software program is allowing blind children to attend local primary and secondary schools using the same textbooks as their sighted classmates. The capacity of these blind children to use a computer not only allows them to turn in their assignments in a form (ink print) that their teachers can read, but it has also helped to improve their English language skills. This year, the first blind students graduated from high school, and this same technology allowed them to take the university entrance exam and to enter university – something that was thought utterly impossible only a few years ago.

Thailand

Blind students in Thailand have always been discouraged from pursuing careers in the sciences, although many have had both the inclination and the ability to do so. Thanks to a new government initiative sparked by the efforts of the Thailand Association of the Blind, this is now changing. One of the tools that is making that possible is a new computer-driven Braille embosser with compatible software that allows graphs, illustrations, and other visual materials to be converted quickly and effectively into readable, tactile images.

Philippines

Today, when one calls his or her credit card company with a question or calls an airline about lost luggage, chances are, the person at the other end of the phone is sitting in the Philippines or in India. Recent progress by ON-NET partners in the Philippines is increasing the chances that the person at the other end of the line is blind. Outsourcing and call centers represent a growing sector of the employment market in the Philippines, and ON-NET and its partners are using assistive technology to place well-trained blind individuals into good paying jobs in these centers.

These are but a few examples of how new developments in assistive technology are leveling the playing field for blind students and those seeking employment. Increasingly, organizations such as The World Bank are showing interest in these technologies, as witnessed by the fact that a number of the bank's new Knowledge for Development Centers are now accessible to blind users. Equally important is the fact that these centers have been made accessible by local blind consultants hired by The World Bank.

China

The newest network developed by Overbrook is not carried out at a regional level, but rather in a country that is as large and as populated as many regions of the world: China. THE OVERBROOK CHINA INITIATIVE was spearheaded by a high-level delegation of Chinese educators and policy makers. This group spent time at Overbrook exploring how technology is integrated into the classroom and into an education plan for every student, including those with multiple disabilities. Shortly after the visit, we were contacted by the Chinese, who expressed interest in learning more about how technology was used as a regular instructional tool within our curriculum.

Wenru Niu, a Chinese-American staff member at the Overbrook International Program, carried out a detailed feasibility study that led to a five-year agreement between Overbrook and the Chinese Ministry of Education. This program will create "centers of excellence" within nine schools for the blind, focusing on the integration of assistive technology as an instructional tool. These schools will, in turn, share their expertise with other educational facilities in their respective provinces. The program is also working with three universities to help fully integrate blind students into mainstream faculties with appropriate technological supports. The program is quite new, but already we can see that when our Chinese colleagues make up their mind to do something, they think big. Most of the schools have now moved technology out of the computer lab and into the classroom where Chinese trainers prepared by Overbrook are helping regular classroom teachers to appropriately integrate technology into their instructional plans. The universities are presently developing support services for students with disabilities and working on the necessary policy changes that will allow blind students to move from the currently restricted curriculum options to study in any faculty for which they meet the academic requirements.

Actively Engaging the Blind User

While the concept of building networks both at the regional and country level has proved quite effective in both expanding access to new technologies and in demonstrating how these technologies can be used in "appropriate" ways to improve education and employment for blind persons in the developing world, it has been the very active involvement of blind users of technology that has been the most critical element to the success of this program.

The ON-NET region advisory committee, which meets regularly to make critical decisions on how resources should be deployed, is made up largely of blind community leaders who are also users of these technologies. Likewise, the cadre of advanced-level regional trainers that ON-NET has built in Southeast Asia over the last eight years consists almost exclusively of blind individuals. The situation is such, not out of "political correctness", but for very pragmatic reasons. Firstly, blind users exhibit a passion for these new technologies that is only infrequently observed at the same level within sighted individuals. Secondly, the blind user-teacher relates to the technology in the same way as his or her student – almost invariably making them a better teacher. Thirdly, when it comes to mounting an argument with regards to policy and discussing investment in these technologies with decision makers, no one is more effective than an articulate blind user.

From the outset, Overbrook's International Program has operated under a consistent set of guiding principles. One of the most significant of these principles requires that training activities employ national and/or regional human resources whenever possible. Foreign staff is thus only allowed to take over when Overbrook and its local partners agree that there are no appropriate local resources available to address a specific topic. If foreign staff is needed, it is most likely composed of International Program graduates from other regions or Overbrook staff. Over the years, many of our International Program graduates have generously offered their time and talents by reaching out to their fellow blind brothers and sisters through our programs. Following my article, there will be the opportunity to read the personal account of one such graduate, Tamas Babinszki. The investment that many Overbrook graduates make in the success of the school's international outreach programs recently caused one graduate to observe, "This really is the blind leading the blind, isn't it?" How right she is, and how wonderfully they lead!

Personal Reflections from Tamas Babinszki, Overbrook
International Alumnus and Trainer

After one of my presentations in Shanghai, in front of about 50 students who were studying special education for children with disabilities, I received an interesting comment: one of the students expressed his surprise at the idea of a blind person being able to achieve so much and do so many things on his own. In a way, I was happy to provide such a testimony, but I was also shocked to discover that my lifestyle, in this day and age, was still questionable. Yet, ten years earlier, before I attended the International Program at the Overbrook School for the Blind, it had been questionable for me too.

At that time, computer education for blind persons was very limited in my native country of Hungary. In fact, most of the curriculum that the Overbrook School for the Blind provided was not available anywhere in Hungary. At Overbrook, I learned how to use computers effectively for my studies and later for employment. The diverse international student body also gave me exposure to how people with visual impairments from other countries address their difficulties. After I returned to Hungary, I started teaching English and Computer Science. At the Hungarian Association for the Blind, I designed a course for visually impaired students who were studying at various universities. At Eotvos Lorand University of Sciences, which was the largest university in Hungary at the time, Computer Science was a mandatory subject for all students; however, the university was not able to provide the necessary resources for visually impaired students. As a solution, my class was accredited by the university, and students could take it as a substitute. The class, which mostly covered the use of computers for blind or visually impaired users in higher education, not only fulfilled a core requirement for the students, but it also gave them a useful tool for their studies.

In the meantime, I worked with the Eastern European Network on Access Technology (EENAT) under the sponsorship of the Overbrook School for the Blind, where I published tutorials on the use of screen readers. In 2000, I moved to the United States, where I have been working ever since as a government consultant, providing Section 508 support and accommodation solutions for numerous government agencies. While working in the United States, I was also asked to join the Overbrook China Initiative to help integrate visually impaired students into higher education within three universities in China.

I believe that most of the work I have undertaken thus far in my career is closely related to the education I received at the Overbrook School for the Blind. Overbrook not only taught me important computer science skills, but it made me and my classmates aware of the difficulties that millions of persons with disabilities face around the world. Based on this first-rate education, I was able to make a living and, more importantly, give back to the global community.

Web Accessibility at General Electric

By Preety Kumar
Founder, President, and CEO, Deque Systems, Inc.

When General Electric (GE) discovered that its website was not accessible to persons with disabilities, it knew that it had to do something about it. There was a simple reason for this: it was not in keeping with the company's values. There were significant secondary benefits to reap. GE recognized that the efficient use of accessibility techniques would benefit its bottom line. Roughly 20 percent of potential GE customers are persons with disabilities. Principles of accessible design increase content discovery and device independence. The rapid convergence of devices that can access the Internet is another reason web operators should not assume the current path of communication between input and output as the only way of interaction. Clearly, increasing market share - especially a loyal customer base - makes a difference. Although the business benefits were alluring, GE's move to make the principal functions of its website accessible supported the idea that diversity is essential and that the company should always pursue technological innovations that support its corporate responsibility mission.

While it is important to note that risk of non-compliance was not the company's principal motivating factor in choosing to make its website accessible, GE understood the importance of becoming compliant with web accessibility guidelines. After all, how does one put a price on reducing legal liabilities and risks? It is very much like an insurance policy: car insurance guarantees that there are no liabilities in the case of an accident.

When one navigates a site, there are almost always pop-ups, plug-ins, and a number of other devices that are activated – anything but a system based around simplicity. GE did have simplicity in its design, and, as a result, a majority of issues on the GE site were not complicated. Missing text equivalents to images made it such that a blind user could not hear much of the content on the homepage. Furthermore, a lack of structure made it such that the screen reader that translates text to speech for the blind would tediously read all the links on every page before allowing the user to skip to the main content – page after page. Forms were also difficult to complete without all the instructions being able to function properly with screen readers. Most frustrating, however, was filling out entire forms and then not being able to submit them without a mouse click. Users of screen readers can only use a keyboard, and persons with low vision were unable to increase the font size and hence could not read the beautiful - but small - print of much of the content. It could have been much worse. We performed an assessment of "priority one" and of "priority two", as determined by the Worldwide Web Consortium's (W3C) web accessibility guidelines. We also made sure that we covered Section 508 and the National Federation of the Blind (NFB) Non-Visual Access Program Requirements, a certification GE was interested in obtaining.

By hiring Deque, an outside consultant who specializes in web accessibility, GE demonstrated that it was very serious about achieving accessibility right. GE's web designers, developers, brand team, and graphic artists were ready and eager to learn about accessibility. Deque started by understanding the GE website structure – what content was coming from templates, what were the other common elements, and what was to be included in the scope of this initial effort. Upon deciding what was in scope, we performed an automated assessment of the GE corporate website. We then conducted testing with assistive technologies to make sure we not only caught the issues that made the site inaccessible, but that we also addressed usability issues. Next, working closely with the GE team, we prioritized issues that made it impossible for persons with disabilities to use the site and identified parts of the site that constituted essential functionality. We worked hand-in-hand with GE operations and content writers to make sure pages were fixed so as not to collide with website changes being made on the GE side. Changes to common elements such as templates, Cascading Style Sheets, and JavaScript functions were thoroughly tested and deployed first. Programming changes were coordinated with GE developers. Finally, after all changes were made, the entire accessible edition was published to a staging server. Upon completion of a regression test, the GE.com website, fully accessible to persons with disabilities and certified by the NFB for Non-Visual Access, was pushed into production.

What were the challenges encountered during the GE implementation? Firstly, GE is one of the best known brands in the world. It has invested very heavily in this brand, which has clearly been conveyed on its website. In order to make the website accessible, significant changes to the look and feel of the site had to be minimized. Unfortunately, it was not as simple as telling GE to "remove this and add that." Instead, we had to work with the design team behind the scenes to overcome a number of challenges and incorporate accessibility into the overall template design. Defining the template early in the design cycle rather than later helped us to ensure that accessibility was built in to every component of the site. Although, as I mentioned earlier, this process significantly changed the look and feel of the site, it helped to propagate the accessibility, which had automatically been built into the template.

Once we had the website up and running, however, we encountered a new set of challenges, the greatest of which was how to maintain a high level of accessibility. The buzz word at this phase in the development was "sustainability." Sustainability is a very difficult goal to achieve, as it requires a constant monitoring process. Unlike the Y2K era when, on the 31st of December, everyone was standing by impatiently to see what – if anything – would happen, only to discover on January 1 that all the anticipation was for naught, web accessibility is an ongoing process. The GE team wanted an easy method of staying compliant and fixing new issues that arise as their website changes. The greatest lesson that we learned is that accessibility is an ongoing process that requires an easily-deployable method of continuous comprehensive monitoring.

We thus remain engaged in a continuous monitoring program with GE to help the company with a variety of accessibility issues that arise on a regular basis. In doing so, we have found that what is most important is "minimizing the noise". In other words, we strive to only surface the new and changed pages, as it makes it easier to implement the required changes.

The general process that we take comprises the following steps:

- *Defining the scope*
- *Performing an assessment*
- *Evaluating the extent, intensity, and nature of the problems at hand*
- *Evaluating the alternatives to fix the problems*
- *Implementing the necessary changes*

The above steps are achieved with the help of tools, as well as with consistent guidance from web accessibility experts. Furthermore, each time we repeat this process, we reevaluate its effectiveness. In is crucial that we constantly identify issues and audit against an established benchmark. What this means is that we must have a baseline in place to know what we are measuring against. Moreover, in order to propagate accessibility, one must standardize the use of accessible templates. In essence, the template is a shell that will carry on, allowing the content to naturally fall into place.

The last major phase in making GE's website accessible was treating the multimedia and embedded content, such as PDF and Microsoft Office documents that existed on the site. We decided to begin the accessibility process with the static pages, then the templates, followed by the dynamic content, and lastly the embedded content. The reason why we saved the embedded content for last was because the pages leading to the embedded content were inaccessible. If one cannot get to the documents, there is no point in making them accessible.

Throughout the project we employed constant, rigorous testing using real-world assistive technologies. I cannot emphasize enough the importance of such testing. Although without automation, one simply cannot achieve the comprehensive, consistent, and repetitive kind of auditing that is necessary, one must also be careful not to neglect the equally valuable tool of experience. We are pleased that, as a result of our work on the GE website, we were able to publish new style and development guidelines for GE, as well as establish a comprehensive accessibility compliance process.

The most common question I get from industry representatives regards the cost of making a large corporate website accessible. Frankly, I think there are a lot of myths about the cost of web accessibility. One must remember that taking an existing website and adding accessibility to the content line is similar to the ratio of buying insurance for a car. In other words, maintaining web accessibility is like purchasing an insurance policy; and it is usually the same cost ratio – not a large amount to add in light of the tremendous benefits that can be reaped as a result.

GE.com is now accessible to an additional 120 million people across the United States and the European Union alone, who would have previously been frustrated and unable to use the website.

Core Challenges and Opportunities for Industry and the Private Sector

This chapter focuses on what contributors to the first G3ict Global Forum have found to be some of the core opportunities for inclusive and assistive information and communication technologies from an ICT industry perspective. These accessibility experts unearth key components that must be taken into consideration when incorporating accessibility into large-scale industry. In this vein, they share their experiences as entrepreneurs, explore industry trends, open source solutions, investment opportunities in the market of assistive technologies, technical challenges in a fast-moving industry and private sector-led initiatives aimed at mainstreaming assistive technology applications in the consumer market.

New Directions for Accessible and Assistive Information and Communications Technologies

By Michael Paciello
Founder and Principal, The Paciello Group

I will be addressing four major topics in my article on new directions for accessible and assistive ICTs. Firstly, I will discuss the direction in which I believe technology is going today. Secondly, I will examine issues that I believe, particularly within industry, can be approached from a governmental and disability constituency perspective. Thirdly, I will define some of the main issues that I feel are barriers to accessibility for the next generation of emerging technologies. Lastly, I will present my notion of forming "alliance strategies" to confront accessibility issues. Working together around alliances, such as those that G3ict has already created, is key to achievement in the accessibility movement. As such, I wish to focus a large part of this article on examining the potential for government to act as a catalyst, how industry can support government, and how alliance collaborations based on trust are the key principles underlying necessary strategies.

In terms of assistive technologies, great strides are still needed in the following four areas: voice I/O (input and output), real-time captioning with voice recognition, open source technology, and something that I call the "third wave of accessibility" – which I will go on to explain in further detail later on.

Voice I/O (input and output), a speech recognition and speech output that we typically associate with screen readers, is the next wave of the future. How it is executed, and more importantly, the extent to which it becomes integral to the IT and ICT environment, is going to be something that will change dramatically over the years. As most of us are aware, in the majority of research labs, as well as on most personal computers, voice I/O systems tend to work "okay." Yet with the research that we will see taking place over the next few years, we can expect great leaps and advances to occur. As part of these developments, I believe that we will see much improved voice recognition systems within I/O systems.

In Chapter 5, Larry Goldberg, Director of the National Center for Accessible Media, emphasizes the importance of patching (improving computer usability) for the deaf and hard-of-hearing, as well as for descriptive videos services. Imagine the ability to integrate such technology across a wide band of media networks. The capacity that does not exist on a human level today can be achieved through human interface on the computing level by employing speaker recognition that automatically listens to, records, and captions media events in real time. Such technology has already been explored in a number of labs. In fact, my first introduction to such solutions was through the United States National Security Agency (NSA).

Open source assistive technology is a valuable aid to all of us in the disability community; and, as we are all well aware, the cost related to the purchase and acquisition of such solutions – particularly personal, assistive technologies – is quite expensive. Someone must pay for it, whether it is a government service organization or a particular organization to which an individual belongs. The notion that assistive technology is readily available to everyone and anyone at any time is something that is very attractive, but is still very much a work in progress.

Already IBM, for example, has given some of its own technology to other organizations to foster this movement – again with the purpose of giving back to the community by providing technology to persons with disabilities without requiring extraordinary financial means to do so.

Then, there is the notion of a "third way to accessibility." This expression refers to a new infrastructure that is truly capable of running across platforms. It does not matter whether the user is working on an Apple machine, a PC, or a Linux platform, because the system is cross platform and multi-vendor accessible. Such infrastructure can thus be implemented in IBM, Apple, Microsoft, Adobe, or in any other company. The "third way to accessibility" denotes an infrastructure which is capable of working within the existing mainstream architecture. It provides a layer of what I call "integrated services" that tie together all of the systems that are simply natural to those within the disability community. Such systems include features such as speech recognition, accelerator keys, access keys, access properties, and synthetic voice – all of which are naturally inherent to those of us with disabilities.

In addition, the "third way to accessibility" also presumes fully accessible data. In other words, with these new integrated systems, the user would no longer have to worry about whether or not the file being consulted or the information that needs to be typed into an electronic form is accessible. The data itself is accessible, and all this is accomplished within a framework that actually acts as a personalized interpreter to the individual on an individual-by-individual basis, disability-by-disability, or ability-by-ability basis.

This is the direction in which I believe we are headed and in which I would like to see us go. Unfortunately, we are a long way from achieving such integration and subsequent harmonization of technology. I would submit that most of these technologies exist in one form or another, and, in many cases, it is just a matter of harmonizing in a logical, coherent, and collaborative matter.

What is clearly missing is the implementation of internationally harmonized accessibility standards. A set of standard accessibility features, interfaces, services, and data that is stored in accessible formats needs to be created. What is required to achieve this?

First of all, we have a very obvious accessibility gap. This means that the emergence of non-accessible technology is growing faster than the development of personal assistive technology for individuals with disabilities. As such, the gap between accessible and non-accessible technology is growing exponentially. The graph to the left maps the gap that exists between mainstream emerging technology and accessible and assistive

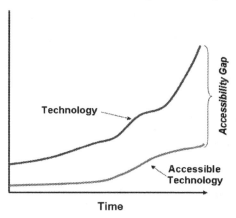

technology. This gap also exists as a result of personal assistive technology adapting or reacting to emerging technology after the fact – and that is a big problem. Ideally, in the development of software, as with any object, it is within the architecture – the conceptual design – where one begins to integrate accessibility.

A long time ago, we learned how to do this from the usability perspective, so we started thinking about user-centeredness in notions of individuals without disabilities. We need to start focusing on accessibility at the architectural level as well, in order to close this gap. As a result of the accessibility gap, persons with disabilities and aging persons lack mainstream technology inclusion. The gap is widening at an increasing pace, leaving those with disability further behind the rest of society.

There are many notable technologies and standards all over the world that are being developed to enable accessibility and/or to enhance emerging technologies for improved usability. The problem is that there is no alignment or cohesiveness to them. There is clearly a lack of harmonization; and the efforts that have been undertaken to try to bring things into alignment with the laws that mandate access to technology for persons with disabilities have been fragmented. The fact of the matter is: we still have a mixed bag and a severe lack of organization.

We also must be careful to avoid the notion of fear-based incentives. I think there is a mindset in the world that says, "If we can file a lawsuit, it will spur others into action." People in industry, scientists, and researchers are aware of the issues that individuals with disabilities face. The more we threaten and propagate this fear as result of lawsuits, the more likely these businessmen, scientists, and researchers will become defensive. We need to think about more proactive and positive ways of attacking the problems that still exist around accessibility at large.

Finally, concentration particularly on those who work with disability constituencies is needed. Furthermore, we must understand what mindset industries work from. A lack of this understanding is a major roadblock in achieving accessibility. Business is about making money and understanding propositions. It is important to recognize that there is a way to make a profit in the accessibility business. There is a maxim that says, "we turn on business investments." We must keep this phrase in mind, because it conveys what is the largest motivator for industry at large.

Lastly, I would like to point out a few strategies that I believe will prove extremely helpful in achieving accessibility. First of all, the establishment of a concrete model is indispensable. TEITAC, the Telecommunications Electronic and Information Technology Advisory Committee, is a potential model for collaboration. TEITAC is a federal advisory committee chartered to enhance the current version of Section 255 of the Telecommunications Act and Section 508 of the Rehabilitation Act. It is made up of 42 different organizations representing the United States government (at both the Federal and State levels), industry, disability communities, and international representation from Canada, the E.U., Japan, and Australia. TEITAC's activities – much like what is taking place within the G3ict initiative – is an exemplary model for collaboration At the first TEITAC meetings, there were numerous agendas that constituents wanted to see achieved. Over the course of several months, however, they came to work together on a common agenda. This is quite a feat, given that committee members had to face some very serious conflicts regarding what to prioritize and what was in the best interest of their respective constituencies. It is a good model, and we hope it will be an example for the world and other global initiatives.

All of the existing initiatives, collaborations, and alliances formed around accessibility rely on one underlying principle, and that is trust. Various constituency groups within government and within industry must trust one another if we wish to reach universal consensus on our common path towards accessibility.

Accessibility and Business Value

By Anne-Rivers Forcke
IBM Human Ability and Accessibility Center

Accessibility is of fundamental importance to IBM; it is part of our corporate commitment to diversity and integral to our core values. Our commitment to diversity and accessibility began more than 90 years ago in 1914, when IBM hired its first employee with a disability. Even then, IBM understood the importance of finding new ways to help the greatest number of people use and leverage the benefits of information technology (IT). As a company, we have been accessibility innovators since the early 1900s, developing the Braille printer, a talking typewriter for blind persons, and, ultimately, one of the best screen readers for the blind. Over the years, IBM has also incorporated a number of practices and policies into our own role as a global employer with more than 375,000 employees around the world and a commitment to reflect the diversity of the communities in which we do business.

We have learned a tremendous amount from employing persons with disabilities, and we incorporate that knowledge into the software, hardware, and business systems that we use internally, as well as into those products and solutions we provide to our clients. Throughout our own accessibility transformation, we are continually striving to improve our understanding of IT accessibility by working with partners like the World Wide Web Consortium (W3C), individuals and advocates from the various communities of persons with disabilities, software developers, and assistive technology vendors. As the knowledge base of industry best practices continues to expand, we will continue to incorporate them by refining our software and hardware development processes and also by applying those practices to help ensure accessibility in the delivery of our services.

From IBM's perspective, our primary goal in participating in G3ict is to further develop the language and the analytical framework of the *business value* of accessibility. That means improving the understanding of the multiple dimensions of value that accrue to or can be recognized by:

> 1) Employers who embrace the accessibility of information and communications technology (ICT) to benefit their employees.
>
> 2) The public, commercial, and non-profit sector organizations who embrace ICT accessibility to benefit their communities, constituents, and customers.

Understanding the dimensions of this business value and bringing a value-based approach into the global accessibility dialogue is a complex task. Before we can have a productive value-based dialogue, we need to establish a common language or framework in which to provide the context for the dialogue. Once this context is established, we can begin to more fully appreciate and account for the value that we each can contribute and receive by embracing ICT accessibility.

Secondly, we hope that G3ict will help increase awareness of the variety of needs for accessibility of information and communications technologies, generating greater awareness of – and access to – resources. To that end as well, an expansion of accessibility initiatives within industry associations and consortia – like the Web Accessibility Initiative (WAI) of the W3C – can provide organizations in the public, commercial, and non-profit sectors with guidance for developing technologies and solutions that are designed to be accessible from their initial conception, instead of having to be retrofitted for accessibility, post-production.

Finally, we look to the G3ict to facilitate collaboration and learning between companies, organizations, and governments around the world, such as those present at the March Global Forum. We are interested in the wide variety of experiences that were represented at the Forum, and we want to share the lessons we have learned in our 93 years as an employer and provider of accessible business solutions. We are pleased to be part of a global initiative that seeks to understand, accumulate, and share best practices as we advance the accessibility of information and communication technologies around the world.

The Missing Link: Financing the Industry

By Barry K. Fingerhut
General Partner, Synconium Partners

I am the managing partner of a new venture capital fund called Synconium Partners. The fund has been formed to make investments in companies that offer products and services that will benefit individuals with disabilities and add ease of use to these markets. We expect that the partnership will help to create a new clearing house of entrepreneurial investment opportunities within the industry. To that end, the goal of the partnership is to produce outstanding investment results for limited partners by investing in products and services that add value to the life of the ultimate consumer.

Based on the analysis that I have done from an investment perspective, what seems to be missing in the market of accessible technologies is an absence of private capital. Such is the missing link that Synconium Partners strives to provide. Private capital has not been very involved in this industry previously. This following list conveys a better idea of the demographics of this market:

- The United States Department of Labor estimates that persons with disabilities have an aggregate current annual income of nearly $700B and $175B in discretionary spending power.
- U.S. adults over the age of 50 are estimated to have over $1.7 trillion in discretionary spending and $17 trillion of net worth

- Over the next two decades, the phenomenon of aging "baby boomers" will cause these markets to converge and expand dramatically.

- The United States Department of Labor reports that the "over 65 segment" of the United States population totaled 36.3 million people (12% of the total population) in 2004. This group will grow to 71.5 million people (20% of the total population) by 2030.

- Older adults experience greater incidence of disability and "ease of use" issues. According to the United States Census Bureau, currently 14 million older Americans (41.9% of the total older adult population) have one or more disabilities.

A very interesting perspective from the point of view of the investment community is that, with some exceptions, unlike the majority of new U.S. markets that have been created through new technologies, significant portions of the assistive technology industry have not. I believe the market is in such a state, because there is no clear path to achieve standards nor a way to garner the follow-up funding from different government agencies, who should be providing services in support of persons with disabilities.

Today, a vast array of federal, state, and local agencies gravitate towards services that are already in the marketplace, resulting in enormous inefficiencies in product and service delivery. In a 2005 Government Accountability Office (GAO) study, for example, 20 federal agencies were described as operating over 200 programs with significant overlap and a large number of inefficiencies.

Additionally, as long as government remains the largest funding source, bureaucratic standards will continue to dictate the current market environment. With very few exceptions, most large companies have come to view the field of assistive and accessible technologies as one of only liability in meeting standards (e.g. Section 508 compliance).

Where we will go from here, and what does the environment look like right now? I believe that spending levels in the United States will continue to increase on the part of the federal government and most state governments. Though the older population is significantly healthier than in the past, the incidence of those living with disabilities is still much higher than those in the general population. With that being said, I think we are about to see a new reality. This new reality would be brought about by the working age population refusing to accept the ever-increasing tax burden – the burden of supporting the older generation. Therefore, the result would be one of two things: either the government's funding and budgets will decline or not grow, or there will be much greater productivity needed in service and product delivery within the private sector.

Therefore, instead of new technologies essentially creating this industry, new technologies will in effect transform the industry. Such a process will improve products and cost productivity, and more capital will need to be invested in developing new products and services. Additionally, I would say that, from the role that I play as a board member of a non-profit human service provider in New York City, I am finally beginning to see evidence of a much more enlightened non-profit attitude towards for-profit operations. In effect, I believe that we are in the very early stages of significant venture capital investment to support these changes and help create a new entrepreneurial phase of development in the industry.

From our perspective, this means that we have several principal areas that we must focus on. The first one is clearly significant: investing in improved product and service delivery in the areas of sight, hearing, and mobility. We are also looking at and hope to invest in companies that have developed new technologies to improve IT and HR productivity for major service providers. The third area is one that I find particularly troubling. Although there exists ease of use markets, many types of funding, RFP opportunities, and significant data collection and mining endeavors that consider all major aspects of the disability community, these activities do not exist in one place. It is important to invest in companies that deploy innovative business models to assess, train, certify, and hire individuals who are on public or private disability support.

A venture capital partnership in the accessibility domain would not be a typical partnership. It would not be a partnership reactive to new business opportunities, but rather a very active partnership. We feel that an initial joint venture with a number of established companies is an ideal step in creating such partnerships.

We are looking at putting together the capital behind all the great technological work that is taking place. Returns on investment are clearly there. The ability to have access to private capital on the part of entrepreneurs is sure to transform the industry and will certainly incite a lot more innovative thinking on the part of both the entrepreneurs and their investors. Furthermore, early success in the field will bring about additional venture dollars, which, in turn, will cause significant changes in the number and diversity of people that the industry is able to serve.

Anatomy of an Industry Success Story: Jaws

By Ted Henter
Director, Henter Math
Creator of Jaws, Freedom Scientific

I have often been asked how Freedom Scientific made JAWS successful. The question is ironic, as one would not want to do it the way we did, as we did it the very long and hard way – without a lot of forethought and without a lot of prior knowledge as to how to go about it. Nonetheless, we were very fortunate that we did it! Along the way, I was able to learn many things about how it should be done, and I would like to present some of those ideas here.

JAWS for Windows came out in 1995 and soon became – and still is – the most widely used Windows screen reader. Almost two hundred thousand people are using it around the world and in close to 20 different languages. Today, JAWS enjoys a dominant position in the market. Again, we did not get there by good planning; we just started working on an English-based screen reader and worked very hard to make it as good as we could. We did so, in large part, because I was the President of the company, and I am blind. It did not hurt that the Chief Technology Officer was blind as well. Because a relatively large number of our programmers, tech support staff, and sales associates were also blind, there was significant internal usage of JAWS, which led to valuable unsolicited feedback about the screen reader. Being a relatively good English-speaking screen reader, we decided to branch out into Europe. Why? Well, that was where the money was.

People in Europe wanted a German-speaking screen reader, a Swedish-speaking screen reader, etc., and they had the money to commission it. Various groups of Europeans approached our company, and we worked in partnership with locals who knew the language and could help us create the best screen reader for their respective countries. We started developing different language versions, and as the product became more successful and as the company became more profitable, we branched out into the lesser developed countries as well.

As we became more well-known and global, however, we encountered significantly more problems in terms of making the computer speech accessible to the various versions of Windows that we were dealing with. We were fortunate enough to be able to talk to developers like IBM that have always been interested in accessibility. Microsoft was also present. Thanks to cooperation from the major manufacturers, we were able to get the "inside scoop" on their software and receive assistance in fixing some issues that were preventing JAWS from accessing embedded information.

One of the most important lessons we learned while developing JAWS was that it is crucial to start with a good core of developers, products, and product ideas in order to create something that works well in one environment. Then, it is necessary to branch out through partnerships in other countries with other languages. Furthermore, Braille must also be readable. Since there are various Braille languages, multiple experts around the world must be consulted.

It is best to have a local developer in each country where the screen reader is sold, who will invest in the translations and other customized changes that need to be made. It is up to those who design the core product to design the screen reader in such a way that these changes can be made in an efficient manner.

The core company or partnership should then monitor the local developers to make sure that proper cooperation is taking place. Nowadays, this form of operations management is much easier to carry out than it was 20 years ago. In resume, those three pieces: the core products, local experts around the world who adapt the product to their particular needs, and the people who provide the information to the local developers, make for a great partnership. Lastly, as I mentioned earlier, user input – both internally and externally – is crucial to the development process as well.

Personally, I do not think having accessibility built in by the company that designs the operating system is a good solution. Doing so would have a negative effect on persons with disabilities around the world, as a lot of incentives would disappear and economic realities would make it such that certain features would no longer be available upon release of the product. In my opinion, the ideal solution to the accessibility issue is to have a viable industry of small developers, such as my company, Henter Math, at times competing and at times cooperating with one another to provide the best access that there is.

Accessibility Challenges and Opportunities over the Web

By Victor Tsaran, Accessibility Program Manager, Yahoo Corporation

Every week when I speak at the new hire orientation at Yahoo!, an interesting thing happens: when I ask the new staff if they have heard of or know anything about accessibility or usability, about 70 percent of people raise their hands and answer in the affirmative. This level of awareness in the private sector is largely due to the introduction of Section 508, W3C guidelines, or simply the dissemination of best practices. People have different reasons for following accessibility – anything from "our CEO told us to do so" to "we had to incorporate accessibility because of the contract requirement." The good message here is that we are living in a better world in terms of awareness about accessibility than we were even 10 years ago when Yahoo! was first started. That is great news.

The not so good news is that accessibility – and I attach the word usability to this as well – is a moving target, which means we may never live in a fully accessible world. The saying goes: "let us make the world a better place." It does not say to make it a perfect one. While advancements in mainstream technology make accessibility more possible and affordable than ever before, this progress also brings about new challenges – touch screens or user-generated content on the Internet, for example.

To achieve better integration of accessibility in the private sector, it is often necessary to exercise a multifaceted approach where various benefits of implementing accessibility are considered depending on the context of the discussion. For example, properly structured web pages, which are also great for search engine optimization, are one of the issues that is most commonly discussed. Search engine optimization is a very fancy term for a simple concept: the better a page is structured, the easier it is for search engines to index it and, in turn, yield more relevant results for a user seeking specific information.

Closed captioning, while being a very useful technology for people with hearing impairments, is also a potentially great enhancement for video search. With data from a closed caption file or a transcript, the search engine can return more precise results about a requested video clip or movie. When the user types in a phrase from a movie or show, the website will tell them exactly what video it is and at what minute the searched phrase was spoken. When elements such as closed captioning and properly structured web pages are combined, accessibility becomes more than a "right thing to do", it becomes a "right thing to have" – more users, more precision, more money.

I would also like to briefly go over some of the challenges that the Internet industry is currently facing as it directly affects companies like Yahoo!

The very first challenge is that technology has an ever-changing nature. The Web is transitioning to new interfaces, new interactive models are being implemented, and the impact of these interfaces on accessibility and usability is not immediately known. Many of us have experienced the latest websites with desktop-like behavior, such as My Yahoo! and Google Maps – with widgets and modules that can be dragged and dropped just as one would on the desktop computer. If the user does not operate with a mouse or his/her screen reader does not understand how to interact with a particular web page, we are faced with both an inaccessible interface and unpredictable user behavior.

Organizations, like W3C, the Mozilla Foundation, and IBM are actively working on the development of new standards and best practices to help developers deliver more accessible dynamic websites; but it will be some time before these standards are adopted by all major browsers and content providers.

The second challenge is that assistive technologies, such as screen readers, screen magnifiers, and voice recognition software, are not readily capable of handling new interfaces. Therein lies another piece of the aforementioned moving target where assistive technologies, as powerful as they may be, do not provide adequate access to new dynamic web interfaces. Even if the latest versions of assistive technology software were up to date with best practices for developing dynamic websites, we would still be faced with the problem of low-income users not being able to afford such costly solutions.

Another significant challenge that we are wrestling with is that there are no ready solutions to address the accessibility of user-generated content. On social networks such as YouTube, MySpace, and Yahoo! 360, where it is nearly impossible to control all the contributed content, we have no reliable technology that would allow us to automatically caption contributed videos or attach alternative text to uploaded pictures. Users are not going to spend time making content accessible if the process is not simple and if there is no incentive to do so. There are some projects that have attempted to fix accessibility through user engagement (e.g. digitizing books by filling out

CAPTCHAs (image verification with audio alternative) via www.recaptcha.net or labeling images with friends via Google). These projects, however, are in their testing phases, and some may never even be released.

The last challenge that I wish to address that is prevalent in companies like AOL, Google, and Yahoo! is the fact that a lot of content that these companies display is not produced by them. Rather, it is the content that they receive from their partners; and their role is strictly to serve that information to the user. To this end, it is the common responsibility of each individual who creates an interface to make that interface accessible.

In conclusion, as I mentioned before, we need to give the users the ability to interact with accessible and usable dynamic content. In order for this to happen, website developers must adopt best practices for rich Internet application development, while assistive technology should learn to make use of such structures.

Accessibility of user-generated content still remains a largely unresolved problem, mostly due to the lack of technology that could help automate the process of resolving accessibility issues or make it easier for users to do so themselves. Some interesting projects from Recaptcha.net, Google.com, and others are attempting to fill the gap by encouraging the user to help address accessibility through collaboration. However, at present, it is difficult to measure the success of such projects.

In the age of the social web, where different websites may share the same content, accessibility should matter to everyone. With so many interconnected web pages, it is easy to imagine how one site's inaccessible content may surface on another fully-accessible site and make it less usable. The new web makes us more connected than ever before, but it also brings with it the shared responsibility for keeping this common space accessible for everyone.

Open and Accessible: New Models for Collaborative Innovation

By Frank Hecker
Executive Director, Mozilla Foundation

The Mozilla Foundation is a non-profit organization that exists on the boundaries between the private sector and the non-profit sector. We grew out of the Mozilla Project, which started with Netscape and then continued with America Online. We are now an independent initiative that comprises a non-profit organization, the Mozilla Foundation, and a for-profit subsidiary, the Mozilla Corporation.

The mission of the Mozilla organizations is to promote choice and innovation on the Internet. We pursue this objective primarily through our product Firefox, an alternative web browser to Internet Explorer (IE) and other proprietary web browsers. Firefox, with tens of millions of users daily, is the second most popular browser in the world after IE. As such, it comprises approximately 10 to 15 percent of the market share in the U.S. Firefox is special in the sense that it is a free and open source product. What this means is that the software's underlying source code is available free of charge to each and every user. To this end, the user can take the software, use it, distribute it, customize it, and build his or her own products on top of it.

As is evident by the nature of our browser, one of the key goals we are trying to achieve as an organization is to keep the Internet truly open. In the Mozilla Manifesto, a document the outlines the guiding principles of the Mozilla organizations, we also emphasize the importance of recognizing the Internet as a global public resource that must remain open and accessible to all. When we say "accessible", we are using the word in the broad sense. In other words, we do not only intend for accessibility to only refer to persons with disabilities, but also to individuals who cannot afford to purchase software or who do not read or speak English and need access to software that supports their native languages.

We promote accessibility to people who cannot afford software by literally giving our software – including its source code – away. Likewise, we help provide accessibility to people using other languages by supporting localization of Firefox into dozens of languages and regional variants. Last, but not least, two years ago, we began promoting the accessibility of our products to persons with disabilities as part of our support of broader accessibility initiatives in the world of open source and free software.

Our first goal is to make Firefox a showcase for web accessibility and, in particular, to meet the challenge of providing accessibility to advanced web applications. Such applications are those, for instance, which Yahoo, Google, Microsoft, AOL, and others are rolling out for the consumer market and that many companies like IBM are developing for the enterprise market as well. These new applications take advantage of new web standards that make it possible to deploy web applications that are as rich as desktop applications.

Our second goal is to extend Firefox accessibility to all major computing platforms – not just to Windows, but also to Mac OS X, Linux, and other platforms, with a particular focus on extending accessibility support to open source platforms such as Linux. Again, one of the advantages of the Firefox product is that it is a cross-platform product. People use Firefox on Windows, Macs, and Linux, and it is our responsibility to make sure that Firefox is as accessible as possible on all of these platforms. We therefore must ensure that Firefox not only runs well on the platform, but that it corresponds to the accessibility standards of the platform and, moreover, that it is able to take advantage of the accessibility infrastructure of the platform: accessibility APIs, screen readers, screen magnifiers, switch access – all of the components of an accessible computer platform.

Even though we are fortunate enough to have a robust revenue stream from the Mozilla Corporation's business ventures, we cannot take on all this work ourselves. After all, we are not a company the size of Microsoft, IBM, Yahoo, or Google.

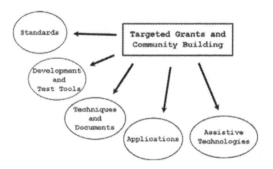

One major way we compensate for our relatively small size is through our open-source developer community. Being an open-source product not only means that the source code is available to everyone, it also means that everyone in the world can participate in the creation of Firefox and its related products.

Our third goal is therefore to expand our pool of developers as much as possible. We are not just looking to expand our traditional

123

developer community – people who are working in the IT field in developed countries and have an interest in open-source software – but also we are looking to expand outside the U.S., the European Union, Japan, and other G8 countries. We also wish to include developers in the disability community, as we see many benefits of having persons with disabilities work on accessibility products. One of the persons that we sponsored to go to the CSUN conference in February of 2007 was a blind gentleman from Australia, who is developing an open-source screen reader for Windows. Since his software is open source, he can now take that project and invite anyone in the world to participate in furthering developing that technology.

The final point that I would like to make is: when we talk about accessibility, it is not enough to look at a piece here or a piece there. We must look at providing a complete accessibility solution that encompasses everything from standards to development software and test tools (which should themselves be accessible) to how-to techniques and documentation on how to do things like create accessible web applications. We must also consider applications like Firefox, accessible web applications that run on top of Firefox and other browsers, and assistive technologies like screen readers and screen magnifiers. If we take advantage of the standards, applications, and techniques that exist, we can provide a fully accessible experience for the end user. In sum, our goal as an organization is to foster these various areas through a combination of targeted grants and community building within the Firefox and Mozilla community and within the broader community of open source developers working on accessibility issues.

Internet for Everyone: Consumers, Businesses, and Governments

By Dr. Emdad Khan
Founder, President & CEO, Internet Speech

Internet Speech is a new start-up company based in Silicon Valley, California. Our technology, Voice Internet, provides access to the Internet without a computer to anyone using any phone with any user's voice. The beneficiaries of our products really do span the gamut: persons with disabilities, elderly persons, people without access to a computer, and highly mobile people, just to name a few. As such, Voice Internet is good for consumers, businesses, and governments alike.

We are currently living in the information age, and in this information age, information is money – just like time is money. As we know, the largest source of information is the Internet, and equal access to this main source of information should be a fundamental right for all human beings. Unfortunately, such is not the case today. While there are over 2.5 billion connected phones in the world today, there exist only approximately 400 million connected computers. In other words, the computer population represents roughly 14 percent of the total telephone population in the world.

In addition to the lack of general access to computers in many parts of the world, it is also difficult for a number of people to learn how to use a computer. For that matter, it can often be quite difficult for people who have been using computers for some time to keep up with new features, such as adware, spyware, registry cleaners, pop-ups etc. However, there now exists an alternative way of accessing the Internet, and that is through a personal device, such as a cell phone or a PDA. These are great devices, but the user interface is very problematic, due to its small keypad and screen. More importantly, the content is very limited – especially for cell phones – given that one would need to rewrite the content using another language such as WML or CHTML to make web material accessible. Since there are over two billion websites, rewriting them all would cost trillions of dollars and thus not feasible.

Even if a simple, accessible computer or personal device were readily available, there would still be millions of people who would not be able to learn to use it. To overcome these limitations, Internet Speech has come up with a solution: providing Internet access by phone. Billions of dollars have already gone into the Internet. Why not maximize this investment by rewriting it such that it is accessible by the masses? At Internet Speech, we have written a software called "Intelligent Agent" (IA) that is intelligent enough to take today's Internet content and deliver it to anyone over any telephone in a manner that is quick, precise, meaningful, easily navigable, and pleasant to listen to. The diagram to the left illustrates the main components of our software.

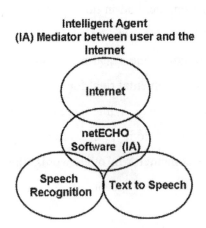

Intelligent Agent (IA) Mediator between user and the Internet

- Internet
- netECHO Software (IA)
- Speech Recognition
- Text to Speech

The intelligent agent netECHO®, as shown to the left, acts as a mediator between the user on the telephone and the Internet. One simply has to pick up his phone, make a phone call, and the agent will ask, "What would you like to do? Would you like to surf, search, e-mail,

netECHO System Architecture

use e-commerce, or listen to music?" Suppose the user responds "surf the net." The agent will then ask him, "website name, please," and he will say, "United Nations" or "Yahoo!" or the name of whichever site he wishes to access. The agent will then download and extract all the text from that page. Listening to all the contents on a given page is good if that page is displaying an e-mail or report. If it is a news site or a page that displays multiple types of content at a time, however, then one does not have time to listen to everything. In this case, the Intelligence Agent will give highlights of the page (called "Page Highlights"), and once the user hears the highlights (usually three at a time), he can select one. The Intelligent Agent will then go to the desired page and read only the relevant story from that page. Such a process directly simulates the average behavior of a user accessing the Internet via a computer: the user looks at a website, clicks on something, goes to the desired page, and reads only the relevant contents. He does not read everything, because he lacks the time and/or the interest to read everything on the targeted page.

The Intelligent Agent renders the content in a short, precise, easily navigable, and meaningful way by using Page Highlights, Language Processing, Matching Techniques, and Artificial Intelligence. The Page Highlights function is similar to the process of page ranking used in search engines. It calculates the highlights based on information, such as font size, boldness, color, contents density, and word meanings. Once the user is on the desired page, the Intelligent Agent finds the most appropriate content by using matching techniques, artificial intelligence, and language processing algorithms.

Not only does voice Internet bridge the digital divide, but it also bridges the language divide. Currently, about 70 to 80 percent of the content on the Internet is in English, meaning that people in countries like China, Japan, and Brazil do not have access to 70 to 80 percent of the Internet. This fact clearly constitutes a "Language Divide." Comparatively speaking, the magnitude of the language divide is quite close to that of the Digital Divide. Internet Speech is able to bridge the Language Divide by using a translation engine that, in real time, translates the rendered contents into another language. If the user says (in any language), "CNN in Chinese" (e.g. Mandarin), the Intelligent Agent will then access the CNN English page contents and convert them into Chinese (e.g. Mandarin) in real time. Now, as far as the language variable is concerned, 100% of the Internet is accessible to most people in the world.

Clearly, Voice Internet is ideal for service providers who provide different voice services. It is also good for businesses and governments, as it enables them to provide special voice services that can be heard over any phone and eliminate the need to re-write the content and create stand-alone interactive voice response (IVR) systems. For example, oftentimes, when a customer calls a bank, she has to answer four or five questions and then listen to a certain amount of content. With Voice Internet technology, the standalone IVR systems are moved into web-based IVR systems, thereby enabling contents from any website to be provided to a computer or to a phone without needing to recreate stand alone IVR systems.

The other key benefit to Voice Internet is its ability to significantly ease accessibility. What accessibility with regards to Internet demands today – especially in light of Section 508 – is that persons with disabilities have access to information on a computer. This objective is good, yet very limited. However, if we extend accessibility to another 86 percent of potential users who have a phone but not a computer, then we are suddenly bringing information to a much larger population through a relatively simple technology.

What are the main challenges and opportunities associated with Voice Internet? The biggest challenge that Internet Speech has encountered is dealing with the new market and new technology. Negotiating a new market or new technology one at a time is much easier than dealing with both simultaneously. Thus, raising funds and building products while trying to achieve market acceptance and growth has been very difficult. However, overcoming such challenges has also spurred significant opportunities.

Firstly, because we have created this technology, we have been able to obtain market leadership with a large market share. Secondly, the return is going to be high in function of our leadership in the market and the niche that our new enabling technology will fill. Third, the current technology will generate several follow-up products, resulting in a long-lasting industry and sustainable business for leading market stakeholders.

I believe that the following policy steps are needed for Voice Technology to have a significant impact:

1. Ensure a low, affordable calling rate when accessing the Internet by phone. In many countries, telephone costs are very expensive, while, in countries like the United States, rates are quite reasonable. In order to ensure that everyone can enjoy the benefits of the Internet, we must first make telephony affordable.

2. Make Voice Internet available to all Internet users. Internet kiosks are great for computer access to the Internet. By simply adding telephones in the Internet kiosks, many people who cannot use a computer will be able to access the same information just by making a phone call.

3. Integrate Voice Internet into computer training to minimize the number of people who drop out of computer training classes due to personal difficulties using a computer.

In conclusion, Internet can be provided to everyone by using any phone and any user's voice, thus truly bridging the digital and language divides and improving education, communication, and the global economy.

Public-Private Partnerships: the European Project ASK-IT

By Nikolaos Floratos
Project Dissemination Leader, e-ISOTIS

Mobility Impaired (MI) persons have a wide variety of functional impairments. Although it should be noted that only 2-3 percent of persons with disabilities are in wheelchairs, any condition that prohibits the free movement of any body part constitutes a mobility impairment. In the context of ASK-IT, the definition of mobility impaired persons requires consideration of a diverse population of individuals, including those who are blind or partially sighted, deaf or hard-of-hearing, illiterate, cognitively impaired or with learning difficulties, unable to walk, have difficulty walking or bending limbs, or have medical problems that affect balance and stamina.

To date, little consideration has been given to a "design for all" philosophy that facilitates inclusion using info-mobility services to benefit the quickly growing market of Europe's senior and special needs populations. Information Technology (IT) capabilities have seemingly infinite benefits to MI users, whose limited mobility yields a consequent need for "assistive" services. Indeed, the need for such well designed IT solutions is much more clear-cut than in any other sector of the European Union citizenship.

To this end, ASK-IT aims to develop an extended ambient intelligence space for the integration of functions and services for mobility-impaired persons across various environments (e.g. car, bus, airplane, home, work, leisure and sport).

Future mobile phones of ASK-IT manufacturers to be used as potential intelligence platforms.

ASK-IT focuses on geo-referenced and personalized transport and tourism services. Emphasis is on seamless service provision, independent of the media being accessed, user location (i.e. indoors, outdoors, in a city, in transit etc.), user type, and residual abilities.

As such, ASK-IT maintains the following as its key objectives:

- Mediation of services and content: in a pervasive, translucent, understandable, and managed way, supporting seamless and efficient supply.
- Seamless environment management: seamless provision of support services everywhere, at any time, and through many mobile and/or fixed means (i.e. accessible in all places, mobile, self-installable, easily interfaced with assistive devices, etc.).
- User preference and context-related driven processes: offering intelligent support and automatic adaptation of service content and layout (user interface) to the users by knowing his/her exact location, transportation plans, static profile (i.e. type of disability, age, gender, etc.), dynamic preferences (i.e. mode of

transportation, hotel preferences, restaurant preferences, etc.), and type of user (i.e. tourist, commuter, businessman, etc.).

- Flexible geo-referenced services: combining provisions for multimodal travel information with pedestrian navigation on accessible routes – both outdoors and indoors – and according to the required level of accuracy by the user (i.e. higher accuracy required for blind users for obstacle avoidance) and the context of use (i.e. more precision required on lane position while driving a car versus riding a bus).

- Maintaining a confidence-based environment for the user: effectively handling issues of safety, reliability, security, privacy, and usability.

Sub-projects Undergone to Prepare an ASK-IT Device

Sub-project 1(SP1): Content for All

Sub-project 1 forms the basis of all the other sub-projects. In this first project, information is collected on the required content, based on user requirements and modeling of the content. The starting point is the identification of the user group and the relevant priority use cases. Surveys and participant observations are carried out to assess info-mobility needs and to identify available products in the market. User requirements resulting from this sub-project are then translated into measurable constructs and qualitative and quantitative measurement methods and criteria. This process will, in turn, produce a strong link between requirements and empirical assessment. The subsequent analysis of all existing content results in a common content format and the development of a semantics-based data management module. The module is what allows ASK-IT to have dynamic access to all gathered content.

Sub-project 2 (SP2): Tools for All

The work in this sub-project focuses on the development of tools, applications, and services being offered to the end user through the Multi-Agent System (of SP3). The tools to be developed include an enhanced accuracy universal localization system (improvement of the level of accuracy in navigation and seamless provision of transportation modes and buildings – both in cities and in rural areas), and an integrated accessible route guidance system. Appropriate interfaces for engaging in the following activities will also be integrated:

- e-commerce and e-payment activities
- vehicle control
- health and social activities
- use of other assistive devices
- e-work
- e-learning

The integrated interfaces will be developed based on intuitive, innovative, and cross-platform-compatible concepts that combine haptic, audio, and visual elements in function of the MI groups' residual abilities.

Sub-project 3 (SP3): Ambient Intelligence Framework

In this subproject, an extended Ambient Intelligence Space (AmI) will be specified and developed for the integration of functions and services for MI users across several environments. The main objective is to allow direct, natural, and intuitive dialogue to take place between various applications and services, providing effective organization and processing of content. The enhanced AmI Space will personalize ASK-

IT services by taking users' preferences, habits, and residual abilities into account in relation to actual situations, thereby supporting MI users in a way that will help them to achieve specific tasks using a variety of interactive devices. This sub-project thus entails the development of a Multi-Agent System for service monitoring and delivery, a self-configuration module for the user interface, the implementation of a semantics engine for knowledge mining and discovery, modules for local and wider area networking, service integration, and security management.

Sub-project 4 (SP4): Accessible Europe

The application of the integrated ASK-IT service will take place in seven pilot sites throughout Europe, in order to test its various functionalities in a wide range of urban and inter-urban (cross-site) scenarios. The test phase will serve to demonstrate ASK-IT's feasibility, interoperability, usability, reliability, and viability, and to propose system improvements, modes of use, and extensions. The final sites and application scenarios per site will be selected according to the available content and requirements from SP1, as well as to infrastructure availability for SP3 modules.

Sub-project 5 (SP5): Horizontal Activities

The general objective of this final sub-project is to correlate the different areas of research that take place in the other four sub-projects. The goal of SP5 is thus to establish a common research framework that caters to activities such as dissemination, exploitation, management, interface based on user feedback, legal and organizational aspects, system architecture, standardization, and policy issues.

Preliminary ASK-IT Applications Pilot Sites

The ASK-IT Consortium consists of more than 50 partners from 15 countries in Europe, representing the following research areas:
- Industry (mobile phone developers, middleware providers, transportation means manufacturers, assistive technology developers, etc.)
- Research Institutes (on transport, psychology, etc.)
- Universities
- Software companies
- Telecommunications companies
- Elderly and persons with disabilities organizations
Project Dissemination Leader: Nikoloas Floratos, e-ISOTIS (Information Society Open To Impairments) Greece, www.ask-it.org
References: This article is based on the public deliverable D5.3.1 "ASK-IT Project Presentation" prepared at the beginning of the project

Harmonization and Standardization: Opportunities for Persons with Disabilities and the Private Sector

This chapter will focus on the role of industry consortia, NGOs, standardization organizations, and international institutions in tackling some of the core areas of opportunities discussed in the previous chapter. By drawing on a number of international perspectives, the authors in this chapter reflect on recent global standardization success stories and current efforts by standardization organizations to determine which success factors should be leveraged to foster harmonization and standardization of key categories of accessible and assistive ICTs. Likewise, the chapter's contributors offer practical suggestions for the fostering of new initiatives and/or work methods that depend on multi-stakeholder participation. Lastly, this chapter illustrates the importance of mass production in achieving affordable accessible technology solutions and, consequently, the importance of standardization and harmonization guidelines to ensure that such mass production can take place.

European Disability Strategy and Accessibility

By Inmaculada Placencia Porrero
European Commission Directorate General Employment, Social
Affairs, and Equal Opportunities

The European Year of People with Disabilities in 2003 brought European citizens to think about disability rights. Although European Union (EU) Member States are mainly responsible for disability measures, the EU regulatory bodies also play a major role in complementing and enhancing national measures, while fostering the conditions needed for further progress.

The Commission's 2003 Communication entitled "Establishing Equal Opportunities for People with Disabilities: A European Action Plan 2003-2010" (COM/2003/650) provides the framework within which the Commission Disability Action Plan will be developed. The framework of the action plan identifies three main operational objectives, which are to underpin the development of the plan in the following successive phases by the year 2010[13]:

- Full application of the Antidiscrimination Employment legislation [14]

- Mainstreaming of disability issues in relevant Community policies and processes

- Improvement of accessibility for all

---

[13] Text of the 2003 Disability Action Plan Communication
http://ec.europa.eu/employment_social/news/2003/oct/en.pdf
[14] Equal Treatment in Employment Directive

To this end, the EU seeks the active inclusion and participation of persons with disabilities in all aspects of society. The EU considers disability to be a human rights issue – not a matter of discretion. This human rights approach is also at the core of the Convention on the Rights of Persons with Disabilities, which the European Community actively supports.

The Commission's 2005 Communication entitled "The Situation of Disabled People in the Enlarged European Union: The European Action Plan for 2006-2007" (COM/2005/604) reported on the achievements in the first phase of the European Action Plan and defined new priorities for the following years[15].

- Encouraging activity including employment and participation in society
- Promoting access to quality support and care services[16]
- Fostering accessibility of goods and services
- Increasing the EU's analytical capacity[17]

The accessibility of mainstream goods, services, and infrastructures has always been a key component of the European disability strategy. Accessibility to information and communication technology products and services has been fostered through the adoption of various policies,

---

[15] Communication on the second phase of the European disability Action Plan http://ec.europa.eu/employment_social/index/com_2005_604_en.pdf

[16] Social services, services supporting deinstitutionalization, assistive services etc.

[17] This provision regards the use of reliable and comparable data to understand the evolving situation of persons with disabilities and their integration in society

as is described in the e-Accessibility Communication of 2005 (COM/2005/425).

In Europe, as in many other places in the world, millions of people cannot fully reap these benefits, while a significant percentage is effectively cut off from them totally. Today, persons with disabilities are estimated to make up close to 15% of the European population. Many of them encounter barriers when trying to use ICT products and services. It is difficult to imagine how persons with disabilities would be able to enjoy their fundamental rights when accessibility to ICT is not a reality.

Access to employment and education, for example, is not possible for persons with disabilities without accessible ICT. The main objective of the 2005 Communication was to promote a consistent approach to e-accessibility initiatives in the Member States based on their voluntary contributions, in order to foster self-regulation in industry. Two years after the publication of the Communication, by the end of 2007, a follow-up assessment on e-accessibility in the various Member States will be made. The Commission may then consider additional measures, including new legislation, if deemed necessary. Regardless of what, if any, legislation is deemed necessary, community action is still the main force needed to ensure the inclusion and participation of all Europeans.

In the 2005 Communication, the Commission fosters the use of three approaches not yet widely used in Europe, as well as reinforces several activities that are already underway. The three new approaches are public procurement, conformity assessment, and exploration of legal measures. I will go on to address each approach separately in this order below.

The revised directives on public procurement contain specific references to using "Design for All" [18] and accessibility requirements as possible criteria for selection among competing vendors. There is a strong need for consistency of accessibility requirements in public procurement in Europe in the ICT domain. The experience in the United States with Section 508 of the Rehabilitation Act has shown the positive influence of public procurement in promoting accessibility. Taking this into account, the European Commission issued in 2006 a standardization mandate for e-accessibility requirements to be used in public procurement[19].

The main objectives of the M-376 mandate are to harmonize and facilitate the public procurement of accessible ICT products and services and to provide a mechanism through which public procurers have access to an electronic toolkit that enables them to make use of harmonized requirements in the procurement process.

When it comes to conformity assessment, possibilities for the development, introduction, and implementation of certification schemes for accessible ICT products and services are thoroughly explored. In the above mentioned mandate, the Commission has asked the European standardization organizations to prepare a report that will

---

[18] Design for All is also know as "Universal Design." There are three main strategies for DFA: 1) design for most users without modifications, 2) design for easy adaptation to different users (e.g. using adjustable interfaces), 3) design with a view to connect seamlessly to assistive devices.

[19] The text of the mandate can be found at http://portal.etsi.org/public-interest/Documents/mandates/m376en.pdf

present an analysis on testing and conformity schemes of various products and services that meet accessibility requirements. Such conformity measures will consider the full range of possible solutions, including supplier self-declaration, certification/accreditation of suppliers, and third party certification schemes.

Naturally, there also must be a thorough exploration of legal measures taken to ensure accessibility. Legislation demanding accessibility already exists in some Member States and in some countries outside of Europe. There is, however, risk of market fragmentation if accessibility requirements are similar, but with small divergences. As such, legislative measures must go from demanding accessibility standards to specifying exact requirements. In Europe, several legislative documents already have provisions which can be used to enforce e-accessibility.

The full potential of this legislation will be explored in order to advance e-accessibility in a coherent manner. In February of 2003, a special working group called Inclusive Communications (INCOM) was established to identify the constraints and problems that users with disabilities face in accessing and using electronic communications in the context of the existing legislation and its use and effectiveness. INCOM also sought to anticipate problems and opportunities related to new and future technologies and applications and suggested changes to the existing legislation

A number of positive actions influencing e-accessibility in Europe have been promoted and supported by the Commission for over 10 years. Designing ICT products and services using the "Design for All" methods from the very beginning ensures that such products can be used by the largest number of people. Avoiding having to "retrofit" accessible solutions is essential for the creation of a sustainable Information Society for all.

Because the European Commission strongly believes that European Standards on e-accessibility would contribute to the proper functioning of a single European market, the Commission continues to support the development of accessibility standards in the ICT domain, while at the same time promoting their implementation and use. The need for global harmonized accessibility standards to enlarge the ICT market has been recognized as a priority by all key stakeholders. Industry experiences a lot of difficulty in addressing a wide set of national – and even regional – standards. To this extent, European standardization efforts on accessibility are very relevant for the implementation of Article 9 of the Convention on the Rights of Persons with Disabilities. Standards remain voluntary instruments that, by themselves, will not solve accessibility problems. Tools to facilitate the use of accessibility standards by industry are also essential in achieving the accessibility goals established by the Convention on the Rights of Persons with Disabilities.

The European Commission supports increased cooperation between key actors, such as disability and accessibility experts, resource centers, users organizations, researchers, industry representatives, and policy makers through a network called EDeAN[20]. The network has a contact center in each European Member State with competence on Design for all and accessibility. This network of resource centers exchange information and educational material in Design for All courses. Furthermore, in order to raise awareness about Design for All, the European Commission issued the first European

---

[20] http://www.edean.org

Awards in "Innovation in Design for All and Assistive Technologies" in November 2004.

The e-Accessibility Communication also recognized the need to set targets for accessibility and monitor progress through in-depth research activities. A preliminary study was issued with the objective of assessing how ICT products and services available in Europe take into account e-accessibility and Design for All. Research remains a key instrument in investigating new technological solutions to address the needs of persons with disabilities and those of older persons. Research within the European Union is funded through various European Framework programs. At this moment, in the 7th Research and Technological Development Framework Program, there is a section entitled "ICT and Inclusion" that addresses disability and aging, among other related topics.

This is a crucial moment for the European disability policy. The Commission is currently preparing the next phase of the Disability Action plan for the years 2008-2009. The Convention on the Rights of Persons with Disabilities, signed by the European Community in March 2007, encompasses the essential elements of the EU Disability Strategy, combining anti-discrimination, equal opportunities, and active inclusion. As such, accessibility remains a key component of the European disability activities and of the Convention on the Rights of Persons with Disabilities.

Specific actions will continue to be undertaken to improve accessibility in Europe. In particular, the work on standardization of accessibility requirements and its international dimension fosters the enlargement of the accessibility market, creating an opportunity for more competitive and more accessible products.

Accessibility Standards for Information and Communications Technologies: The Japanese Experience

By Dr. Hajime Yamada
Toyo University, Japan, Chair of the Standardization Investigation
Committee for Improvement of Accessibility Common to Areas of
Information Technology and Software Products

I would like to devote the following article to discussing how to facilitate the use of ICT accessibility standards. Japan already has a series of ICT accessibility standards in place. The name of the standards is: "Guidelines for Older Persons and Persons with Disabilities: Information Communication Equipment, Software and Services", of which there are five distinct parts:

Part 1 – Common Guidelines; developed in 2004

Part 2 – Information Processing Equipment; developed in 2004

Part 3 – Content; developed in 2004

Part 4 – Telecommunication Equipment; developed in 2005

Part 5 – Office Equipment; developed in 2006

During the development of these standards, one of the most important elements our Standard Development Committee considered was stakeholder involvement. We invited user communities, industry, academia, as well as government agencies to develop these standards. In some cases during the development, there were conflicts among stakeholders, which we saw as necessary to the process of developing accessibility standards.

Next I will cover how to facilitate the use of these standards. The reason why it is important to emphasize the facilitation of standards is very simple: standards are only effective if they are applied in the market. In other words, if we develop a standard that no one uses, then that standard is clearly useless. Therefore, we must develop standards that can widely be applied in both mainstream civil society, as well as in industry.

The first strategy that the Standard Development Committee introduced called for the inclusion of elderly persons. In Japan, 20% of the population is over the age of 65. This figure is big enough – and consequently attractive enough – for manufacturers to consider its implications in the market. If we were to only develop standards to benefit persons with disabilities, it is likely that private sector stakeholders would consider the market benefit to be too small. As a result, we must look to the other 90%+ of the population as well. If we then add the 20% of the population that is elderly, suddenly we are talking about a consumer base that accounts for 30% of the entire national population. How could firms not take a market that size seriously? Therein lies our strategy! That is not to imply, however, that we do not strongly believe in the inclusion of elderly persons in the information society in and of itself. On the contrary, we feel that digital inclusion of elderly persons is necessary – independent of our efforts to achieve accessibility for persons with disabilities.

The second strategy was to develop standards that could be implemented globally. In my opinion, global applicability "wakes up" industry and is thus necessary for both national and foreign deployment. To this end, we submitted Japanese industry standards to various international standardization organizations in order to achieve global harmonization, as well as to make any necessary revisions to our national standards. We first sent our common guidelines to the International Organization for Standardization (ISO), who has already started the final voting process. We hope to achieve international standard status by the end of 2007.

Following ISO approval, the information processing equipment and office equipment standards will go to ISO's JTC1. JTC1 also has a working group on accessibility that contributes to the development of two documents, namely user summaries and inventory of standards. These two documents will be approved by the JTC1 soon next year. It is in this way that we will enter into the international arena. When I was working as a project editor on the convergence of Japanese national standards with international ones, I found that input based on different views from different cultures significantly improved the quality of the resulting synthesized standards.

The third strategy to turning national standards into global standards was to consistently participate in international, regional, and national activities. For instance, in the United States, there exists a standard for procurement developed by the Telecommunications and Electronic and Information Technology Advisory Committee (TEITAC). In response to this standard, my European colleagues and I are now submitting information to the TEITAC committee and other various committees on information in order to achieve global harmonization in the area of procurement. Naturally, this is just one example of an area where we are seeking the development of harmonized standards.

One important possibility to foster faster adoption of standards is to use government bargaining power and public procurement such that accessibility standards can be used as a requirement for public procurement. However, more encouragement is necessary in this field. One positive solution and strategy would be to develop a United Nations ICT Accessibility Product Award. Awards and other forms of encouragement can help the industry to consider this issue more seriously.

In this presentation, I explained the trends in accessibility standard development and use of these developed standards. Not only in Japan but also in United States and Europe, accessibility standards are being developed. The next step is facilitating the use of these standards so that people including persons with disabilities and older persons can enjoy the benefit of informatization of the society.

The Importance of Harmonization: Perspectives from the Information Technology Industry Council

By Ken Salaets
Executive Director of Access Standards and Director of Government
Relations, Information Technology Industry Council

The Information Technology Industry Council (ITI) membership spans the globe and includes companies such as Canon, HP, IBM, Microsoft, Panasonic, and makers of the Blackberry and various devices.

The committee has been very active in working on an array of issues and in multiple areas of collaboration. Since products are made for the customer, there is no incentive for new product development without taking a customer's needs into consideration. It is therefore indispensable that ITI constantly evaluate how the industry is doing in the marketplace and continue to actively solicit feedback from various stakeholders through forums and organized events.

Why is harmonization so important? There are a few key aspects to cover when discussing harmonization of standards. When we design global products for the global market, the idea is that we can build once and then sell everywhere. The advantage of this process is that, for all people – whether they have a disability, an age-related limitation, or are uncomfortable with technology – we can focus on investing our resources in meeting the needs of the consumer, rather than on meeting the needs of regulators and administrators. Naturally, there is significant cost that goes into the process of trying to meet regulations and meet administrative requirements – labeling requirements and the like. Essentially, every time a border is crossed, one is faced with a new requirement that implies significant cost. In some cases, the number of lawyers who work for a manufacturer outnumber the number of people in the company's design and development team. These hard-to-swallow facts are important to keep in mind when considering the importance of standardization on several fronts.

If we were able to build and sell everywhere, however, we could easily justify the cost by spreading those costs over a wider market. The end result would not only be cost-effective for manufacturers, but it would also be cheaper for government, who could much more easily implement new products alongside other products that were meeting the needs of its "consumers" – the citizens. Then ultimately, of course, it is also cheaper for consumers, as it generates competition.

When we have a standard that is both global and widely respected, it creates an infrastructure that enables manufacturers to innovate beyond that standard; and it is in that innovation – that aspect of product development – that one finds competition. Competition is often key in creating additional options for the end-user, as well as for driving down cost. Furthermore, it motivates standards and harmonization, while also allowing small businesses to compete in the marketplace.

Many of the world's greatest innovations were created by people in sheds, in garages, and at kitchen tables. Innovation can occur on many levels and often on an individual basis. If there were a standard platform upon which innovators could develop and design products, there would undoubtedly be significant more innovation in the marketplace.

With regards to harmonization, ITI is an organization that belongs to, participates in, and is supported by a number of groups. We also house the Secretariat for InterNational Committee for Information Technology Standards (INCITS), which is one of the IT standards development organizations in the United States. Furthermore, we participate in the JTC1 Special Working Group on Accessibility and have produced very critical resources for industry and for government, such as the User-Needs and Standards Inventories.

ITI has also succeeded in identifying what we refer to as a "gap analysis", which is the identification of additional standards that must be developed to address the international marketplace. Furthermore, ITI has the privilege of participating in the Global Industry Standardization Association (GISA), which includes the Arctic Information and Communications Technologies Assessment (AICTA) from Europe, JAILA from Japan, and the Consumer Electronic Association from the United States. GISA addresses an array of issues from climate change to digital television to accessibility.

ITI, along with GISA and the trilateral group (Europe, United States, and Asia) plans to propose that industry create an industry inventory of best practices relative to accessible ICTs. The reason why such an inventory is so important is because one of the key driving elements in the marketplace is peer pressure. If companies like Hewlett Packard, Microsoft, Canon, Oracle, and SAP are looking over each other's shoulders, it drives the marketplace and, consequently, a more consistent approach to accessibility. If we can expand this driving mechanism into other parts of the world where we have now launched regulatory standards processes, industry and consumers are sure to benefit.

Media Leading the Path to Providing Accessible Information and Deploying Harmonization and Regulations

By Larry Goldberg
Director, Media Access, WGBH Boston

The focus of this article is access to media worldwide, with an historical viewpoint dating from 1955 to 2012. The media is a key component of ICT, as is evident by the attention it is given in the Convention on the Rights of Persons with Disabilities – both with reference to access to culture and access to technology.

A good starting point is the origins of captioning in the United States. Captioning began in 1955 when the United States government started funding the captioning of 16 mm films that were disseminated to deaf clubs around the country. At the time, this was the only formal way that any form of dynamic or electronic media was made accessible to deaf and hard-of-hearing persons. In the early 1970's, the open captioning of television began at WGBH, the public broadcaster in Boston. The captioning of "Julia Child's French Chef" and the ABC Evening News led the way, with the captions "open" and visible to everyone. Closed captioning had not yet been invented at the time.

In 1980, however, closed captioning was launched with the help of federal funding and the engineering assistance of the PBS and ABC TV networks.

With the advent of closed captioning, TV watchers were able to choose whether or not they wanted to see captions. Federal funding was also beginning to be supplemented by corporate support and advertisers throughout the television industry. Even so, the growth of captioning remained slow on both local television stations and cable networks.

In 1990 – the same year that the Americans with Disabilities Act was passed – the Television Decoder Circuitry Act was approved by Congress and signed into law by the first President Bush with the hopes of inciting more pervasive captioning. After the U.S. Congress approved the act, the Federal Communications Commission (FCC) crafted the complementary regulations. In 1993, those regulations began to have a very strong affect on the marketplace. From that time forward, any television set sold in the United States that was 13 inches or larger had to possess built-in closed caption decoder technology. Such a provision was intended to both grow the market for captioning and to make captioning more widespread. Moreover, essential to the evolving nature of media technology, one section of the law said, "As new video technology is developed, the Commission shall take such action as the Commission determines appropriate to ensure that closed-captioning service continues to be available to consumers." As a result, the caption decoder law was future-proofed for the emergence of digital television.

Despite these measures, however, captioning did not become pervasive or even commonplace among the most successful cable networks and local broadcasters.

In 1996, appropriate regulations were once again considered when the "Telecommunications Act of 1996" revamped United States regulation of television and telephones. A little-noticed provision was added to that law, which required that all television programs become accessible via captioning after a certain period of time. The clause was aimed at serving deaf and hard-of-hearing persons in particular, though the needs of blind persons were also considered. The FCC closed captioned programming regulations were progressively phased in from 1998 to 2006, resulting in the present status, as of January 1, 2006: virtually 100% of television programming in the United States transmitted via broadcast, cable, and satellite television must now be closed captioned.

During the rapid growth of TV closed captioning, WGBH began developing a closed captioning system for movie theaters. This system, called "Rear Window", was officially launched in 1997. Captioning for movie theaters is purely voluntary, as no federal regulations explicitly require it. As such, theatrical captioning has only reached a small percentage of the movie theaters in the United States and Canada – 300 installations as of mid-2007. In addition, since its launch, more than 500 films have been closed captioned for theatrical release.

In the year 2000, the United States government procurement regulations, known as "Section 508", established a requirement for the captioning of all federal government-created or -funded media. However, in both the FCC regulations and Section 508 procurement requirements, what is missing is a captioning requirement that sets minimal levels of caption accuracy and quality.

At the time of this writing (September 2007), the FCC has a pending rulemaking on the quality and reliability of closed captioning. The deaf community has clearly expressed that the quality of the captioning they rely on, particularly for live programs, is below minimum standards.

"Real-time" captioning is what is employed for live shows, sports, news, and other non-scripted productions.

Another looming problem is captioning and other forms of media access in new emerging media platforms, such as HD-DVD, Blu-ray DVD[21], and high-quality technologies for interconnecting media devices using connections like component video and HDMI[22].

None of these new developments are assured of proper caption delivery and industry representatives, as well as government agencies, are only just beginning to address these new media access concerns. There is particularly high consumer interest in the areas of accessible online and mobile device media. Clearly, much work needs to be done to assure the accessibility of these devices as well. A federally-funded research project began at WGBH in the fall of 2007 to begin to tackle the issues of caption provision in mobile media devices such as cell phones, PDAs, iPods, and the like.

Digital cinema is another fast-moving media delivery platform where accessibility is under development. Film projectors are being replaced throughout the world by digital servers and projectors. Opportunities for advancing accessibility – and barriers preventing it – are both presented as the film industry moves rapidly into the digital realm.

The catalyst for all of this progress over the years has been voluntary industry efforts spurred by consumer advocacy and – of course – government funding and regulations triggered by acts of Congress.

---

[21] Next generation optical disk format
[22] High Definition Media Interface

In addition to the widespread attention to and concerns about closed captioning for deaf and hard-of-hearing persons, it is also important to address video description for blind and visually impaired individuals.

While most Americans are familiar with closed captioning in the United States, video description is not as well known. Video description is a service for blind and visually impaired persons that provides added narrated descriptions of what is not seen in video, delivered as a second audio program service on television, on DVDs, in movie theaters, and on the Web. It is widely available in the United States, Canada, and the UK – on public broadcasting stations and some commercial services as well. In Canada and the UK, a small percentage of digital television programming must be transmitted with video description; in the U.S., video description is provided via voluntary efforts funded by the government and domestic networks.

Video description in the United States first began in 1985 when stereo television was invented, employing the Multichannel Television Sound (MTS) standard. The specification for MTS includes support for not only left and right channels of audio, but also for an extra channel called the "secondary audio program." With the growing availability of stereo+SAP TV sets, video description was first launched in the United States at WGBH, with training from the Washington Ear and with funding from the United States Department of Education. The following is a sample of video description taken from the movie "Forrest Gump":

Video description:
A young woman in a white uniform opens a magazine
and starts to read.

Forrest:

"Hello, my name is Forrest, Forrest Gump."

Video description:

The girl starts to nod and returns to the reading.

Forrest:

"You want a chocolate?"

Video description:

She stares at him and shakes her head.

Forrest:

"I can eat a million and a half of these. My Mama always said life was like and box of chocolates. You never know what you're gonna get."

Video description:

His mouth is stuffed with sweets, and Forrest grins at the young woman who ignores him.

In the United States, language-encouraging support and promotion of video description was included in the Telecommunications Act of 1996 (which also mandated 100% captioning). In 2000, the FCC decided to require video description as their interpretation of the intent of the Telecom Act. However, after completion of the FCC's rulemaking process, the requirement was brought to Federal court by industry trade groups who opposed the mandate under the argument that the FCC had exceeded its jurisdiction by establishing a mandate of four hours of video description per week on the major broadcast and cable networks. The requirement was only in place from April to November of 2002, before it was overturned by the court based on the jurisdiction argument.

Video description continues to be supported today by public broadcasters and the CBS and Fox broadcast networks. There is currently a bill in Congress to reinstate the video description mandate by explicitly giving the FCC the jurisdiction that the court determined they lacked in 2002. In addition, R&D efforts are being made today to deliver the audio of video described programs via new technologies and platforms such as HD radio, satellite radio, and other audio services in the near future.

It is interesting to look at what other countries are doing in the realm of captioning as well. In the United Kingdom, for instance, 70% to 95% of programs must be captioned. In addition, national annual quotas call for eight percent of the programming in the United Kingdom to contain video descriptions. Furthermore, the United Kingdom requires that sign language appear on four percent of national programming by 2015.

Throughout the world, individual governments and regional alliances such as the EU continue to examine media access regulations and take steps to make closed captioning and video description more available. In Japan, for example, the Ministry of Public Management has set a target of having 100% of feasible programs captioned this year – for both live and pre-produced programs. In Mexico, there also exists a requirement for captioning. The country is, however, still waiting on necessary funding for the technology development needed to create and deliver captions. In Australia, where there are captioning requirements for both analog and digital television, the target for captioning on prime time is 70% of all programming from 6:00 a.m. until midnight. A number of other countries are also working on requirements for captioning and description, all of which result from government mandates with some cooperation from the local and national media industries as well.

Access to media is being demanded by persons with disabilities all over the planet, not only to the content on television and the web, but wherever and whenever media exists. For persons with disabilities, services like captioning and video description are not just desired, they are required to assure that all people can learn, work, and be entertained equally.

The World Wide Web Consortium Accessibility Initiative

By Judy Brewer
The World Wide Web Consortium (W3C,) Director of the Web
Accessibility Initiative

I am very pleased to be involved in the Global Initiative for Inclusive Technologies. Speaking on behalf of the World Wide Web Consortium, which is the leading industry technology standards organization for Web technologies, we are excited to participate in this initiative and to contribute our feedback based on our experience with the World Wide Web Consortium's Web Accessibility Initiative.

The World Wide Web Consortium (W3C) is a vendor-neutral industry consortium which promotes the evolution, interoperability, and universality of the Web. When the term "Web Accessibility" was coined, we found that many of the provisions needed for accessibility were already goals inherent in existing W3C guidelines. W3C's Web Accessibility Initiative, which has been in existence for ten years now, addresses cross-disability user requirements, meaning that it considers the needs of people with visual, auditory, mobility, speech, and cognitive disabilities, as well the needs of the aging population, who often face functional barriers in accessing the Web.

Clearly, the Web is one of the core resources in many countries that enable citizens to participate in different aspects of society, including education, employment, information access, healthcare services, civic engagement, social networking, and so forth. If people cannot access the Web, a great barrier is created. This lack of access to such a core resource is very appropriately identified in the Convention as a form of discrimination.

What many do not realize, however, is that the Web has the ability to be even more accessible than many other parts of society. A large part of the Web Accessibility Initiative's premise revolves around this very fact. We strive to bring together all of the different stakeholders from industry, the disability community, government, accessibility research institutes, and universities, in order to reach consensus on how to make the Web accessible. To that end, we develop guidelines for accessible websites, browsers, media players, and, lastly, for the software that is used to produce accessible content. To this end, we also review all new advanced technologies for the Web. For example, we began with HTML and have since expanded to looking at XML as well. Since there is so much dynamic web content online, it is necessary to establish accessible rich internet application guidelines to ensure that this content is accessible.

How does one get an accessible Web, and what are the ingredients needed to do so? Firstly, we must look at the role of the web developer. Web developers often use authoring tools (software that helps create websites) when designing or managing web content. Oftentimes, evaluation tools are also employed to assess the accessibility of the content as it is being created. This method, which is employed throughout the entire web design and development process, is by far the best way to assure accessibility.

It is also important to consider what takes place on the users' side. Users often rely on a form of assistive technology to access the Web in accordance with specific needs that vary on an individual basis.

They might, for instance, require a tool that highlights certain sections of a webpage to avoid being distracted by other sections. It is also likely that the user will interact with the Web using a browser and a media player. If this is the case, both the browser and the player not only need to be accessible, but they also must be able to interact seamlessly with the user's assistive technologies. If the technologies cannot inter-operate successfully, the situation becomes very problematic.

At W3C, we strive to develop guidelines that inform the developer's side by taking into consideration the authoring tools, the browsers, and the media players that are being used, as well as the content that is being created. We hold all of these components accountable through various technical specifications. For those who are unfamiliar with what is meant by "technical specification" in the digital world, the term essentially refers to HTML, XML, and other language systems that come into play every time the Web is accessed. W3C technical specifications have been reviewed from the earliest stages of development to ensure that accessibility is supported on all levels and that accessibility information can be carried throughout the site as needed.

W3C has three different sets of accessibility guidelines. The set of guidelines that most people are familiar with are the Web Content Accessibility Guidelines, which explain how to make websites, web content, and web-based applications accessible. The remaining two sets of guidelines are equally important in making the Web accessible. Firstly, there are the Authoring Tool Accessibility Guidelines, which address the accessibility of software used to develop web content so as to ensure that persons with disabilities are able to build websites and add content to the web as easily as any other user. These guidelines also support production of accessible content. It is important to note that, if there were more tools that automatically supported the production of web content, we would no longer need to read the web content guidelines every time we developed a site. The final set of guidelines are the User Agent Accessibility Guidelines, which address the accessibility of browsers and media players, as well as their interoperability with assistive technology.

W3C has both 1.0 and 2.0 versions of Web Content Accessibility Guidelines (WCAG). The 1.0 version incorporates ATAG, the Authoring Tool Guidelines, and UAAG, the User Agent Guidelines, both of which reflect W3C standards that were completed at least several years ago. Currently, we are also developing a 2.0 version of each of these guidelines. The Version 2.0 web content and authoring guidelines provide accessibility for more advanced web technologies, resulting in increased accessibility for persons with disabilities. These guidelines will also be able to be more precisely testable, which is key in assuring that accessibility standards are met.

In addition, W3C engages in ongoing review of technology. At present, we are reviewing all the W3C technical specifications, as well as a number of external specifications, that are undergoing development. As a part of this review process, we develop technical solutions for specific needs, such as dynamic HTML, AJAX, etc., which are covered by the accessible rich internet application document that we work with known as WAI-ARIA.

164

If everyone is essentially using the same definitions of what web accessibility is, then we are already at a great advantage. By referring to a common group of desired standards, we can accelerate the progress of web accessibility and create a unified market for improved authoring evaluation tools and enable re-use of training resources. Common standards eliminate the occurrence of conflicting requirements, which can be very difficult for developers, and also allows consistent monitoring and efficient progress assessment. I cannot emphasize enough the importance of multi-stakeholder involvement and consensus in promoting web accessibility. Without such consensus, building awareness, assessing current levels of accessibility, and establishing an updatable policy framework as technology advances would be very difficult to maintain. The ultimate goal is to establish policies that point to more advanced specifications, which, in turn, spur more advanced guidelines. The ideal sequence of events is to train developers, implement guidelines, evaluate outcomes, and monitor progress.

W3C produces educational materials that have proven helpful to individuals interested in looking at how to make the web accessible in their respective regions of the world. Such information addresses ways to raise public awareness about the need for web accessibility, as well as how to develop adaptable policy frameworks for ever-changing technology. Needless to say, the World Wide Web Consortium is very encouraged to see such a collaborative effort taking place to create harmonized standards that will pave the way towards greater ICT accessibility for persons with disabilities throughout the world.

More ample information can be found on our homepage at w3.org/wai.

Consumers and Accessibility Standards: the European Perspective

Chiara Giovannini
Program Manager, European Association Representing Consumers in Standardization (ANEC)

The mission of ANEC is to ensure the highest level of consumer protection and, in doing so, to ensure public interest representation in standardization. Essentially, ANEC exists to counterbalance the industry view. Certainly standards are valuable tools for achieving public policy objectives. However, at ANEC, we believe that, while standards can address accessibility issues and reliability of ICT services, they are not the only tools by which to achieve accessibility. The following account outlines ANEC's experience with standardization and the consequent lessons learned.

ANEC is very active in representing consumer views in the Web Accessibility Initiative of W3C. We also monitor JTC1 activities on accessibility. As a European association, we follow most intently accessibility activities at the European level. To this extent, we plan to soon begin work on the European Commission Mandate on e-Accessibility and Public Procurement in the ICT Sector.

The European Telecommunications Standards Institute (ETSI) standards on access symbols are one example of our contribution to the development of accessibility standards in Europe. These standard published access symbols serve to indicate to consumers the very basic accessibility features that a number of ICT products and services can support. An example of such a feature is sign language or audio description that can be useful to consumers with a number of different disabilities. ANEC believes that this kind of information should greatly interest public procurers and hopes that industry will choose to adopt the use of these symbols on many ICT products in the near future.

Our experience has led us to realize that there are currently several challenges with consumer participation in standardization processes. To begin with, accessibility standards are oftentimes informal standards, meaning that it can be very difficult for a consumer's voice to be heard. Stakeholder balance in standardization working groups is also a significant issue. Although most of the industry is participating in standardization, there are very few consumers being consulted. We must assess consumer priorities, which, unfortunately, will only be possible with increased budget availability. In this regard, technical expertise, budgeting, and time are all needed to influence standardization, and the lack of all three is clearly the most problematic aspect for stakeholders in standardization committees.

Standardization is essential in implementing Article 9 of the Convention on the Rights of Persons with Disabilities. As I mentioned at the beginning of this article, standards – however essential – are not sufficient in and of themselves to achieve accessibility. Why? Because there are already many accessibility standards that have yet to be implemented, due to the lack of a strong implementation mechanism. Moreover, public funding for consumer participation is needed. In order to implement Article 9, ANEC recommends the proposal of implementation mechanisms that are contained in a legislation tool. In order to accomplish this task, however, national legislation will have to provide sufficient incentive for implementation of accessibility standards.

In fact, regardless of the status of deliverables for which guidance on e-accessibility has been made available – as an International or European Standard – its use remains voluntary. Lack of compulsion is the heart of the problem. The e-accessibility standard can itself represent a state-of-the-art solution but, if it is not attractive to the majority of those who should implement it, it will not be used. As such, standards should not be seen as a replacement for legislation, but, rather, as a complementary tool.

How Can Legislators and Regulators Foster Innovation, Harmonization and Compliance

This chapter consults experts from around the world on the topic of legislation and regulation of accessible information and communication technologies. Contributing authors include representatives from international institutions, national governments, access boards, and academia. Each author presents his or her own perspective with best practice examples in order to provide recommendations for legislative and regulatory enforcement. Likewise, the chapter sheds light on a number of regulatory and legislative challenges and proposed solutions that are applicable to the implementation of the Convention on the Rights of Persons with Disabilities.

ICTs and Parliaments: Opportunities to Foster Legislation Supporting Accessibility

By Ambassador Anda Filip
Director, Inter-parliamentary Union

I would like to address this topic from the perspective of parliaments and the role they can play when it comes to legislation and enforcement – fostering greater awareness, innovation, and compliance for ICT accessibility. I will also discuss the work that the Inter-Parliamentary Union is doing in this area.

For those who are not familiar with the IPU, it is a global organization of national parliaments, which has been around for over 100 years. The organization has primarily served as a forum for dialogue, interaction, and cooperation among legislators from around the world on issues of mutual interest and concern. Having developed standards and norms in the areas of parliamentary democracy and fair elections, the IPU has found itself naturally lending quite a bit of attention to the question of accessibility – including accessibility for persons with disabilities.

In order to develop sound policies, it is important for parliaments and members of parliament to engage as willing and active partners. This premise is a good one, given that parliaments are eager to make the most of the opportunities provided by ICTs. Current statistics show that almost every parliament in the world uses ICTs, a finding that reflects very recent development. In 2000, approximately two-thirds of national parliaments had their own website. By 2006, more than ninety percent of parliaments had published a website on the

Internet, often following the IPU's own guidelines on good practices for parliamentary websites[23].

Parliaments are using ICT for two main purposes: first, to be more transparent, accessible, and accountable to the public, and thus improve their outreach to the constituents that they are elected to serve, and second, to be more effective in their parliamentary processes. To give several concrete examples: In Vietnam, the parliament is preparing to publish draft laws on its website so that citizens can comment on them and thereby have their input taken into account during legislative process. In Austria, the Electronic Law system offers one continuous electronic production channel for legislation. As such, all stages of a law, from the proposal to promulgation, can be tracked via a fully transparent process. This system is designed to invite greater involvement by citizens in the legislative process. In very practical terms, it is also calculated that the new system will save sixty tons of paper annually, which amounts to a savings of more than one million Euros. The question, of course, is to what extent these tools are accessible to persons with disabilities – and here, there is quite a lot that still needs to be done.

Now that the Convention on the Rights of Persons with Disabilities has been formally adopted, the IPU is moving ahead, in cooperation with UNDESA and OHCHR, with the finalization of a *Handbook for Parliamentarians* to analyze and explain the main provisions of the Convention. At the same time, the handbook will address practical

---

[23] Inter-Parliamentary Union (2000). Guidelines for the content and structure of parliamentary Websites. Available at <http://www.ipu.org/cntr-e/web.pdf>

issues, such as how a State becomes party to the Convention, the ratification process, the legislative aspects of implementation, and responding to questions such as:

- What are the main steps to be taken towards early ratification?
- Can the Convention be implemented directly at the national level?
- What new legislation is needed?
- Which laws need to be reviewed?
- How can the main principles of the Convention be reflected in a state's constitution?

Each chapter concludes with a checklist for Parliamentarians, outlining the types of measures that they as lawmakers can undertake in order to:

- Implement the provisions of the convention;
- Ensure that national strategies are in place for the; promotion and protection of the rights of persons with disabilities;
- Make the necessary budgetary allocations;
- Allow Parliaments to exercise their oversight function to enforce relevant legislation in this field.

The Handbook, as I mentioned earlier, is still being developed and, before publication, will be reviewed by an editorial board, which includes a group of prominent members of parliament with extensive experience in the disability field – some of whom are themselves persons with disabilities. Once finalized, the Handbook will be:

- Launched at the global level at one of the IPU Statutory Assemblies;
- Submitted to all national parliaments, with the recommendation that it be translated into the national language and integrated as a tool in the work of the legislative body.

On a case by case basis, we also envision starting a series of training sessions and seminars, at the national and regional levels, so as to assist in building capacities and implementing the provisions of the Convention.

As a practical recommendation, we seek to ensure that Article 9 on accessibility is well covered and accompanied by a menu of good practices and policy recommendations, with a particular focus on:

- Promoting appropriate forms of assistance and support to persons with disabilities to guarantee access to information;
- Promoting access for persons with disabilities to new information and communication technologies and systems, including the Internet;
- Promoting the design, development, production and distribution of accessible ICTs and systems at an early stage, so that these technologies and systems can become accessible at minimum cost.

Another tool that the IPU believes can be used in promoting inclusive ICTs is the new Global Center for Information and Communication Technologies in Parliament. The center was launched in November 2006 in Rome, under the joint auspices of UNDESA and IPU, as one of the tangible outcomes of the second phase of the World Summit for the Information Society (WSIS) held in Tunis.

The idea behind the Global Center is to help parliaments and their members, especially in developing countries, to acquire and effectively use the most advanced information and communication technologies (including, but not limited to, the Internet). Moreover, the Center is designed to help parliaments to improve their internal work methods, as well as to help afford citizens more direct access to their elected representatives. To this end, the center's principal objectives are:

- To improve the capacity of parliaments with regards to their constitutional functions, the law-drafting process, and general parliamentary procedures;

- To increase citizens' access to parliamentary activities and documentation;

- To increase the level of international cooperation among parliaments;

- To increase the coordination of the international community in supporting ICT in parliaments and other legislative development issues.

The Global Center therefore intends to act as a catalyst and clearinghouse for information, research, innovation, and technology, as well as a hub for technical assistance. We feel that the lessons learned within parliaments over the past 10-15 years regarding the implementation of ICT-related projects have the potential to form a tremendous knowledgebase when introducing or developing ICT in parliaments in developing countries.

In providing a framework for pooling information and resources, the Global Center has the ability to link the broadest possible number of initiatives in this field. We also wish to collaborate with other organizations to identify relevant ways and means by which to integrate the commitment to inclusive ICTs, into the work of the Center.

Legislation as a Tool to Implement Accessibility Requirements

By Tamas Babinszki
Accessibility and Section 508 Consultant/Assistive Technology Analyst,
Project Performance Corporation and the U.S. Patent and Trademark
Office

In order to efficiently follow the initiatives of the Convention on the Rights of Persons with Disabilities, it would be beneficial for all governments to make their legislation include mandatory accessibility standards. Legislation is the most powerful tool available to implement accessibility requirements; and, clearly, mandatory legislation is more effective than voluntary standards, because compliance can only be ensured by the former.

In developing countries, where there are people without the basic necessities of food and clean drinking water and where technology has not yet penetrated the economy, many wonder what difference mandatory accessibility could possibly make. Certainly, the concerns are real, and accessibility standards would not matter if the conditions were to remain unchanged. However, there is a great advantage to mandatory standards in developing countries: the earlier accessibility is in place, the easier it is to implement inclusive policies without future difficulties. If accessibility-related legislation is already in place when technology is first imported, the methodology of developing information and communication technology (ICT) will be well established from the start. Furthermore, knowledge will be gained from the experiences of other countries where technology was introduced and developed before accessibility standards existed. The developing countries, advancing technologically with standards already in place, would not have to continually alter standards and remake products, as did their predecessors when faced with new standards. As such, the burden imposed on the economy by trying to change what is in existence to meet standards would be avoided entirely.

In the United States, the difficulties of not having standards in place from the beginning was quite problematic, to say the least. Many technologies were already in place when Section 508 standards became mandatory, meaning that a large number of products and development procedures had to be redeveloped and redesigned after the fact. Furthermore, the methodology of development had to be updated to reflect the necessary changes, which would make products compliant with Section 508 standards. One of the major difficulties for development companies was that products that were developed before 2001, but updated later, had to contain accessibility features. While this change placed a significant burden on the developers of these products, products that were designed after 2001 did not have to face this challenge, as they had been required to include accessibility from the beginning.

To provide effective accessibility requirements, we need to sort our legislation by two criteria: type of accessibility standards and placement of these standards. In other words, we must determine what kind of accessibility standards will be applied and what the scope of their implementation will be.

If we are looking for existing legislation to determine which standards should be applicable, harmonization and globalization of standards should be taken into account. The advantage, especially in developing countries, is that a lot of the hard work has already been done by many developed countries. We can implement standards that were already tested and proven successful, thus leading to the achievement of globalization and the harmonization of accessibility standards. In the long-run, this method of harmonization will not only make future work easier, but by implementing similar standards in different countries, there will be more resources to evaluate experience and make future modifications as needed. The more countries use the same standards, the more governments can contribute to the future development of accessibility.

As with safety regulations, accessibility should be applicable throughout the entire nation. Enforcement, especially in places where it is difficult to comply with standards, should not be penalizing, but rather supportive of the different governmental and corporate agencies. There are many ways in which governments can work with these various agencies to help them comply with legislation. For example, agencies could receive a certain grace period with regards to the time they are allowed before they must comply with legislation. The length of the grace period should, of course, be realistic and reflect the country's overall ability to achieve compliance. Another form of government support should be encouragement of accessible product development. Furthermore, governments could motivate agencies by awarding contracts to those who are the most accessible.

With the groundwork in place, the next step would be for governments to recognize organizations by doing business exclusively with those who meet accessibility standards. Ideally, the ultimate goal would be to extend accessibility requirements to all non-governmental entities.

Accessibility-related legislation not only benefits a community with disabilities, but it also benefits the organizations who comply with legislation. Among many advantages, more methodology is added to the development procedure to increase efficiency, and more business opportunities become available as persons with disabilities are able to use more products.

For the last four years, I have been the head of the Section 508 technical team at the United States Patent and Trademark Office. We have developed very strict policies for contracts and procedures in accordance with the legal requirements. Contracting developers must attend Section 508 trainings, for example. As is mentioned in Article 9, Section 2.h of the Convention on the Rights of Persons with Disabilities, development teams are trained to start incorporating Section 508 requirements from the beginning of the development process. In the testing stages of the development life cycle, all products must pass Section 508 testing.

We discovered one benefit of implementing standards from an early stage when a contractor, who had recently completed Section 508 training with us, started implementing accessibility at the beginning of his design process. The contractor actually saved money by adding Section 508 to his development procedures. He found that the best way to incorporate Section 508 standards was to create reusable code and development templates. This helped speed up the development process by making it more efficient. In the long run, this organization benefited from this new process, and its websites and software were Section 508 compliant and accessible.

In sum, I suggest that developed countries with advanced legislation on accessibility provide support to developing countries, who are in the process of creating their own accessibility-related legislation. This best practice sharing will enable developing countries to be most effective by benefiting from the work in accessibility that has been done so far. In this sense, developing countries have a great advantage over countries who already have accessibility standards in place. There exists an enormous wealth of lessons that have been learned about accessibility thus far; and these should undoubtedly serve as the core building blocks for further improvements.

Establishing Accessibility Standards through Legislation and Regulation: the Experience of the United States Access Board

By Timothy Creagan
Senior Accessibility Specialist, Technical and Information Services,
Access Board, United States

[This article is taken from remarks given during a panel presentation at the First G3ict Global Forum at the United Nations, New York City on March 26, 2007] These remarks focus on the work that the Access Board has done in promoting accessibility in the realm of information communication technologies.

What is the U.S. Access Board, and what does it do?

The U.S. Access Board is an independent agency of the United States government, created in 1973, to ensure access to federally funded facilities. The formal name is the "Architectural and Transportation Barriers Compliance Board," but it is more commonly known as the "Access Board." The Board promotes access for persons with disabilities by developing and maintaining accessibility standards and guidelines for the built environment, transportation vehicles and vessels, and electronic and information technology products. Examples of standards and guidelines developed by the Access Board include the ADA Accessibility Guidelines (ADAAG), the ADA Accessibility Guidelines for Transportation Vehicles, the Electronic and Information Technology Accessibility Standards, and the Telecommunications Act Accessibility Guidelines, to name a few. Likewise, the Board provides training and technical assistance on these and other requirements.

What authority does the Access Board have to develop standards and guidelines for electronic and information technology and telecommunications products?

The authority for the work the Access Board does originates from laws passed by the United States Congress. Four different laws are involved. The first two are the Americans with Disabilities Act and the Architectural Barriers Act, which apply to vehicles, vessels, buildings, and facilities. The remaining two apply to telecommunications products and electronic and information technologies: the Rehabilitation Act of 1973 and the Telecommunications Act of 1996.

Pursuant to Section 508 of the Rehabilitation Act of 1973, as amended, 29 U.S.C. § 794 (d), the Access Board is authorized to issue and publish standards setting forth a definition of electronic and information technology and technical and functional performance criteria necessary to ensure that electronic and information technology allows individuals with disabilities (whether they are Federal employees or lay citizens) to have access to information and data that is comparable to the access of information and data by individuals without disabilities. These standards, known as the "Electronic and Information Technology Accessibility Standards," were issued in December 2000 and became effective as of February 20, 2001.

The authority granted to the Access Board to develop design criteria for accessible telecommunications products comes from the Telecommunications Act of 1996, 47 U.S.C. §255. This law required the Access Board to develop guidelines for accessibility of telecommunications equipment and customer premises equipment in conjunction with the Federal Communications Commission. The Access Board developed guidelines specifying what makes telecommunications products accessible and then the Federal Communications Commission (FCC), a separate Federal Agency, promulgated those rules to enforce the law. The Telecommunications Act Accessibility guidelines were issued by the Access Board in February 1998 and became effective on March 5, 1998.

What work is the Access Board currently engaged in that addresses the harmonization and standardization of accessible technologies?
The Board is conducting a fresh review and revision of the standards, which address how to make electronic and information technology and telecommunications products accessible under Section 508 of the Rehabilitation Act and Section 255 of the Telecommunications Act. To this end, the Board has organized an advisory committee, the Telecommunications and Electronic and Information Technology Advisory Committee (TEITAC) to review standards and guidelines, as well as to recommend changes. The goal of the TEITAC is to produce a consensus report of recommendations, which will then be presented to the U.S. Access Board as a basis for updated accessibility standards and guidelines.

The committee is composed of members from various stakeholder groups, including industry, consumer, assistive technology, and international representatives, among others. The advisory committee meets to discuss proposed changes and revisions to the standards and guidelines. Committee members bring their technical expertise in various national and international design standards to the work of the committee. Members of the committee are encouraged to consider performance-based technical standards from around the world that could effectively be incorporated into the consensus report. These standards are then considered as the committee drafts its report of recommendations for the Access Board. Once the TEITAC has completed its work, the Access Board uses the recommendations as the basis for drafting a Notice of Proposed Rulemaking (NPRM). The NPRM is published in the Federal Register for public comment prior to the issuance of final standards and guidelines. During the advisory committee process – and afterwards – the aim of the Access Board is to develop clear, consensus driven, testable, and reliable accessibility requirements. The Access Board is thus committed to facilitating the harmonization of accessibility requirements to enhance accessibility for persons with disabilities around the world.

Where does the responsibility lie for ensuring conformance with the provisions of Section 508 when a Federal agency acquires electronic and information technology?

The electronic and information technology accessibility standards under Section 508 apply to federal agencies when developing, maintaining, procuring, or using electronic and information technology. The Access Board develops and promulgates the standards; however, since there is no central enforcing agency, each Federal agency is responsible for compliance with the standards. Requiring officials and contracting officials within a particular agency are responsible for ensuring that the technology used in that particular agency is conformant with the requirements of Section 508.

What statements has the Access Board made concerning the need for harmonized standards for accessibility?

The answer to this question and the conclusion to this article is best presented through a quote from Marc Guthrie, a public member of the

Access Board, taken from his remarks at the International Workshop on Accessibility Requirements in Brussels, Belgium on October 21, 2004: "We agree that what is needed is clear, consensus-driven, testable, and reliable accessibility requirements. In this world of global scales, it is critical that accessibility requirements be harmonized throughout the world. Product manufacturers want to build to a single set of requirements – or at least not be faced with competing world wide requirements. We should do what we can to facilitate this, because ultimately if we can make the regulatory process easier to achieve – and by that I do not mean that we need to weaken the requirements that exist today – we will enhance accessibility for persons with disabilities worldwide."

Enforcing ICT Accessibility Rules

By Peter Blanck
University Professor & Chairman of the Burton Blatt Institute at
Syracuse University,
Co-Director of the University of Trondheim e-Accessibility Project

Nagging Questions

Twelve years ago, a White Paper for the Annenberg Washington Program entitled: "Communications Technology for Everyone" (Blanck, 1994), proposed five vital precepts that still are relevant today:

1. Accessibility must be designed in, not "bolted on." Universal design benefits all users, not merely those with disabilities. Government role has yet to be defined in encouraging (perhaps mandating) universal design and in setting standards.

2. Technological accessibility is critical in today's society. The international information infrastructure must not be off-limits to persons with disabilities.

3. Technology enhances educational and workplace inclusivity through individualized curricula, supported communication, schools and jobs without walls, and other innovations.

4. Accessible technology offers opportunities for health care reform, while telemedicine brings doctors to geographically isolated people. With regards to welfare reform, telecommuting helps reduce chronic unemployment and underemployment among people with severe disabilities.

5. Technological accessibility problems exist not only for persons with disabilities, but also for all underrepresented individuals in society – the poor, the isolated, and the vulnerable.

Dialogue, research, and law and policy reform continue to be needed to address and optimize solutions to these issues. A central question from years ago remains posed; whether the inherent design of the Internet's (aka World Wide Web) information infrastructure acts as a barrier or bridge to helping persons with disabilities and other underrepresented individuals move closer to full participation in society (Blanck, in press).

Equal access to the Internet by persons with disabilities, as the gateway to the new global marketplace, to medical information, education, and to the world of work, has been at issue in the U.S. since the late 1990s. In 1999, the National Federation of the Blind (NFB) sued America Online (AOL), alleging AOL's Internet browser was inaccessible to the blind and did not comply with the accessibility requirements of Title III of the Americans with Disabilities Act (ADA) (Blanck & Sandler, 2000). In 2000, the AOL lawsuit and the applicability of title III's provisions to private Internet sites were the subject of congressional hearings, in which it was suggested that the Internet was a "place" of public accommodation appropriately covered by title III (ADA Hearings, 2000). Soon after, the AOL litigation settled and AOL agreed to make its Internet browsing software compatible with screen reader assistive technology accessible to the blind.

A review of these hearings (Blanck & Sandler, 2000), and subsequent legal and policy challenges, identified the importance of

Internet (web) access for persons with disabilities. NFB and other groups and individuals have examined the accessibility of Internet service providers and websites. But the application of Title III's access requirements to private Internet websites remains unsettled.

ADA Title III prohibits discrimination against persons with disabilities in places of public accommodation, that is by private entities offering goods and services to the general public (ADA, 2000). To this end, the law covers conduct affecting commerce directed at the public, including communication and trade within and among states, and between a foreign country and a state. Places of public accommodation include sales and service establishments, and places of entertainment, recreation, and education. However, at the time of the ADA's passage, cyberspace was not yet conceived of as a "place" of public accommodation.

Discrimination under Title III also includes the failure of a private entity to ensure effective communication with individuals with disabilities – unless doing so fundamentally alters the nature of the services provided or results in an undue burden (Blanck, Hill, Siegel & Waterstone, 2005). As an alternative to providing full accessibility through the Internet, title III entities often suggests offering services in other formats, because web access is not readily achievable. For example, an e-commerce retail company may choose to make its services available through a telephone help-line or offer print catalogues in Braille format. Yet, Title III requires the alternative help-line to be staffed in a way that is equal to the services provided to customers without disabilities via the company's website – which may be costly relative to general website access. It remains to be determined whether such alternatives are full and equal.

Beyond the shadow of the law, there are practical reasons for accessible private Internet sites and services. When accessibility is considered a component of a corporate e-business plan, the goods and services become available to millions more people with sensory, physical, cognitive, mental, and other impairments in the U.S. and around the world (Sandler & Blanck, 2005). Moreover, when universal design principles underlie online goods and service provision, they become available to the widest possible customer base – with or without disabilities. By creating a universally-designed e-commerce platform, not "separate but equal" websites as with text only sites, e-businesses cultivate brand and consumer loyalty and reduce the costs of retrofitting sites.

Litigating Access to the Internet

In the area of equal access to the Internet for persons with disabilities, my colleagues and I continue to engage in complex litigation using the Americans with Disabilities Act; however, this litigation often remains more contentious than it should be. This is because, as mentioned above, there is a huge potential market share available to web-based retailers and others from the consumer segment, including persons with disabilities, and indeed a competitive loss from not affirmatively addressing the needs of these consumers.[24]

In the pending and widely publicized United States legal case, the National Federation for the Blind (NFB) versus Target Stores, the plaintiffs prevailed from a preliminary ruling by the court that they

---

[24] See articles in support at http://bbi.syr.edu.

could proceed to demonstrate that the Target website was not accessible. However, the argument needed to be made under circumstances where purchases at Target's physical stores were linked to Target's website activity (that is, the legal case could not proceed on the issue of the accessibility of the website in and of itself). In the case of a blind customer, for example, who regularly buys items via the target.com website and then goes to collect them at the Target stores, there is a clear relationship or nexus between the physical store and the website, and thus litigation could be brought under the ADA.

In the United States, as well as abroad, such legal questions have far-reaching implications. Interestingly, other anti-discrimination disability laws, like those in the United Kingdom and Australia, have written into their legislation that the web is covered as a place of accommodation regardless of whether there is a nexus to a physical store. The next generation question in the U.S. is whether those retailers who do not have physical store locations, but sell solely off the web, are covered by the anti-discrimination ADA law as well (Blanck, in press).

On the international front, there is another important issue pending. In the United States, there was a recent case decided by the U.S. Supreme Court that held that the foreign company Norwegian Cruise Lines, when docked in United States waters to pick up passengers, are covered by the ADA. Therefore, these ships were required to be accessible and have accessible services for persons with disabilities (e.g. ramps for those using wheelchairs). The next generation question from this line of reasoning will be whether foreign entities doing business in United States "cyber waters", as a kin to the Norwegian Cruise Lines case, will be required under the ADA to make their websites accessible for use by persons with disabilities (Blanck, 2007).

Closing

It makes economic sense to make websites accessible to all persons – those with and without disabilities. Oftentimes, litigation in this area is over a broader legal principle; yet major corporations should be aware of the additional market share opportunities that are available if a website is accessible to consumers with disabilities. It is my hope that in short order, the points of dispute will be muted in light of this growing economic reality. The important issue remains as to whether website accessibility, in the absence of litigation, may be integrated into American and other countries' policies as part of the new generation of disability anti-discrimination laws around the world.

A broad approach to ICT access, design, and technology embodies concepts of "universal design," and enables individuals across the globe to have full access to the services and programs of public accommodations (Blanck, et al., 2005). Increasingly, companies with corporate cultures that understand the relation of universal design and market share growth generate value from universally designed technologies to attract business and consumers around the globe (Schur, Kruse, & Blanck, 2005; Schur, Kruse, Blasi & Blanck, 2007). There now exist related and fundamental laws and conventions that unite countries in their pursuit of policies to improve the equal status of persons with disabilities (Reina, Adya, & Blanck, 2006). As such, an understanding of e-access and universal design will help nations to better effect disability antidiscrimination legislation and enhance global markets (Blanck, 2005a, 2005b, 2005c; Quinn, 2006).

References

Americans with Disabilities Act of 1990 (ADA), 42 U.S.C. §§ 12101–12213 & 47 U.S.C. § 225 (2000).

Applicability of the Americans with Disabilities Act to Private Internet Sites ("ADA Hearings"). (2000, February 9). Hearing Before the Subcommittee on the Constitution of the House Judiciary Committee, 105th Congress.

Blanck, P. (in press). Flattening the (In-Accessible) Cyber World for People with Disabilities, Assistive Technology Journal.

Blanck, P. (2007). ADA's Application to Foreign-Flagged Cruise Ships In U.S. Waters: Spector v. Norwegian Cruise Lines, in Disability and Human Rights in Europe; Olivier Deschutter & Gerard Quinn (eds.), Bruyant Publishers (forthcoming).

Blanck, P. (ed.) (2005a). Disability Rights. London, UK: Ashgate Publishers.

Blanck, P. (2005b). Americans with Disabilities and their Civil Rights: Past, Present, Future, University of Pittsburgh Law Review, 66, 687-719.

Blanck, P. (2005c). The Burton Blatt Institute: Centers of Innovation on Disability at Syracuse University, Syracuse Law Review, 56(2), 201 – 32.

Blanck, P. (1994). Communications technology for everyone: Implications for the classroom and beyond. The Annenberg Washington Program, Washington, D.C.

Blanck, P., Hill, E., Siegel, C.D., & Waterstone, M. (2005). Disability Civil Rights Law and Policy: Cases and Materials. St. Paul, MN: West Publishers.

Blanck, P.D. & Sandler, L.A. (2000). ADA Title III and the Internet: Technology and Civil Rights, Mental & Physical Disability Law Reporter, 24(5), 855 – 59.

National Federation of the Blind ("NFB") v. Target, Corp., No. C 06 – 01802 MHP, 2006 WL 2578282 (N.D. Cal., Sept. 6, 2006).

Quinn, G. Achieving eAccessibility: The Role of Equality Legislation and Other Measures. 'The Potential Offered b y the Equality Approach.' Working Paper, 2006.

Reina, M.V., Adya, M., & Blanck, P. (2007). Defying Double Discrimination, Georgetown Journal of International Affairs, 8, 95 – 104.

Sandler, L. & Blanck, P. (2005). Accessibility as a Corporate Article of Faith at Microsoft: Case Study of Corporate Culture and Human Resource Dimensions, Behavioral Sciences & the Law, 23(1), 39 – 64.

Schur, L., Kruse, D., & Blanck, P. (2005). Corporate Culture and the Employment of Persons with Disabilities, Behavioral Sciences & the Law, 23(1), 3 – 20.

Schur, L., Kruse, D. Blasi, J, & Blanck, P. (2006). Corporate Culture and the Experiences of Employees with Disabilities (submitted to Industrial and Labor Relations Review).

Legislative Developments: New Opportunities for the Disability Movement

By Yannis Vardakastanis
President, European Disability Forum

The European Disability Forum (EDF) is an umbrella organization representing more than 50 million persons with disabilities in the European Union. It is first and foremost a human rights organization, founded on the principles of non-discrimination and equal opportunity. Established 10 years ago by a group of individuals with disabilities and family members of persons with disabilities who were unable to represent themselves, EDF began to defend the interests of persons with disabilities in the European Union institutions, including the European Commission, the European Parliament, the Council of the European Union, and all the other relevant authorities.

Before the adoption of the Convention on the Rights of Persons with Disabilities, accessibility was purely a wish, a demand, a desire, and a dream. Now that the Convention has been adopted, accessibility has become a fundamental right, recognized as such in Article 2 (Definitions), Article 9 (Accessibility), and Article 21 (Freedom of Expression and Opinion and Access to Information) of the Convention. Access, usability, and affordability of information and communication technologies by persons with disabilities are not concessions; and the continued exclusion of persons with disabilities from equal access to ICT had now been clearly identified as a form of discrimination.

Given its global nature, there is a need for a common vision on ICT. Common international goals must be defined and implemented through accessible design, production of accessible ICT equipment, and related services for persons with disabilities. There is no doubt that the adoption of the Convention presents a tremendous challenge to the world disability movement, which will have to redefine its way of acting, of merging different plans of action, and of forming strategic alliances. Accessibility must be considered in view of the Convention, which must, in turn, be used as a platform to establish and carry out a worldwide campaign to promote legislation, regulation, enforcement, and compliance.

Now that accessibility has clearly been identified, rights cannot be left to voluntary exercises. It is a great opportunity for all actors to put together a worldwide initiative with, for, and by disability rights organizations to promote a new era in accessibility – with regards to ICT and all other areas covered by Article 9 of the Convention.

EDF has undergone significant action in Europe with regards to accessibility and non-discrimination. In 2004, we decided to launch a campaign to create the link between the funding provided by the European Union to its Member States and the principles of non-discrimination and accessibility. This key campaign concerns the European Structural Funds, which for the period of 2007-2013 account for more than 336 billion euros. Almost 44 billion euros are distributed every year through the Structural Funds to EU Member States. Many regions of the European Union utilize this funding as the main source of public funding. It is therefore a tremendous source of public investment in the 27 Member States. Our demand during this campaign was very simple: "From words to deeds, let's stop the rhetoric about accessibility and take action."

Thanks to our intensive work with the campaign, Article 16 of the Structural Funds General Regulation states very clearly that all the projects that will be funded from 2007 to 2015 should respect the principle of non-discrimination and the accessibility criteria. EDF is now working at the Member State level to make sure that what has been incorporated into regulations will become a reality. To this end, monitoring and implementation processes will be carried out through the deployment of accessibility training programs, accessible ICT solutions and related infrastructures, and transportation systems – to name a few – which will yield tangible improvements in the lives of for persons with disabilities in many EU countries.

In conclusion, both the role of public authorities and the role of the State are indispensable. Legislation, regulation, and, of course, enforcement of these regulations are absolutely crucial to making society accessible. Lack of accessibility is a democratic deficit. Accessibility is therefore a political issue; and it is the duty of the State to guarantee that rights are respected and that persons with disabilities can exercise their rights fully. In the context of the disability movement, it is a tremendous challenge to create broad alliances with public authorities, industry, trade unions, and other stakeholders who support the full implementation of Article 9 – and other provisions of the Convention, for that matter – without any restrictions. The Convention will produce change not only for this generation, but for the subsequent generations as well. It is therefore the duty of this generation, within industry, among policy makers, and through the disability movement at large, to create the necessary provisions and requirements for the success of a paradigm shift in the way society perceives persons with disabilities.

Critical Issues for Developing Countries in Implementing the Convention on the Rights of Persons with Disabilities

By Dipendra Manocha
Assistant Project Manager, DAISY for All Project, DAISY Consortium
Honorary Director IT and Services, National Association for the
Blind, New Delhi, India

I would like to devote this article to addressing what I feel are several critical issues that developing countries are facing today in the implementation of standards and in the formation of rules and regulations. In the context of these critical issues, I will elaborate on some examples of how a number of problems have already been tackled. In doing so, I will draw particular attention to the key strategies employed in resolving such challenges.

I will begin by addressing some critical issues that we are currently facing at the DAISY Consortium. As we know, there are standards such as the W3C Standards for Website Accessibility and the DAISY Specifications defining standards for accessible digital multimedia content. Most of these standards, however, presume a certain existing level of access to technologies for persons with disabilities. For example, it is presumed that when a person with blindness or low vision visits a website, he or she has access to screen reading software. As such, specifications are laid down for expressing web page constructs in a way that assumes and requires the presence of screen reading software.

In developing countries, however, we need to take a step backwards, due to the fact that there is no TTS (Text to Speech) software available in most local languages. As a result, even if web pages comply with the W3C web accessibility guidelines, there is no screen reading software that can read or speak the sites aloud in local languages.

Thus, alongside accessible standards in ICT, we also need to address additional challenges in developing countries. TTS technology is one of the basic technologies used in many accessibility solutions – not only for blind persons, but also for persons with a range of other disabilities, who, due to permanent or temporary conditions, cannot read normal print. For instance, someone who is driving or someone who can no longer use his or her reading glasses would find the text-to-speech application extremely useful. The main issue that needs to be addressed related to TTS software concerns standard API (application programming interface).

Many efforts to develop TTS software in local languages are being made, yet the aspect of complying with international API is often ignored in these projects. TTS is not a piece of software that can be used on its own, rather access software, such as screen reading software, needs to interact with TTS engines to provide the complete solution. If the API of the TTS is not standardized, then every access technology solution will have to be tweaked to be able to use the specific TTS. Unfortunately, this scenario is virtually impossible, as we cannot realistically expect companies who produce screen reading software in the United States to make adjustments to its software such that it is usable with all different kinds of TTS software being developed in remote corners of the world in remote languages. Instead, there needs to be an effort, preferably in the open-source domain, for development of TTS engines in local languages that adhere to API standards, such as SAPI (Speech Application Programming Interface) or SSML (Speech Synthesis Mark-up Language)

Another basic technology that is extremely important for access solutions is OCR (Optical Character Recognition) software. This software allows creation of digital text by scanning. Both TTS and OCR softwares have been available in the developed world since the 1980's, but have yet to be adapted for most languages in developing countries.

Another important issue impeding persons with disabilities in developing countries is the cost of the technology.

Generally, income level in a developed country is six to ten times higher for a similar job in a developing country. Naturally, this ratio is offset by the fact that the cost of living (e.g. food and housing) is much cheaper in developing countries than in developed countries. However, as opposed to the cost of basic amenities, such as food and transportation, technology is actually cheaper in the United States than it is in many developing countries. For example, if I wanted to purchase a copy of the JAWS screen reading software in India, I would have to pay more than in the United States, due to transportation charges and other kinds of overhead that can be incurred in importation.

Likewise, a basic computer would cost less in the United States than in India. Furthermore, in many developed countries, insurance companies or the Government Funds pay for assistive technologies[25].

There are many examples of subsidy: Citizens of the UK can benefit from assistive technology from RNIB by paying 25% of the cost. Students of higher education with disability in the US, Germany, and other Western countries can get equipment such as Braille note taker or Braille display at highly subsidized cost or funded by their respective governments.

However, in developing countries, due to the lack of social security systems, expenditures on assistive technologies must be incurred by the individual with a disability or his or her family. Furthermore, in developing countries, governments often – and rightfully so – spend most of their resources on meeting fundamental needs, such as providing drinking water, two meals a day, and basic education to all citizens.

Despite these challenges, there have been a number of good practices that have successfully been applied in tackling some of the aforementioned problems. The cost of any product is directly dependent on the quantity produced and sold. When we apply this basic economic principle to developing countries, we realize that it favors consumer markets in these nations, due to the large number of potential consumers who live there. Up until now, however, this large potential market has gone virtually untapped. For example, for any given software sold in the United States, there could easily be potential to sell a hundred times more copies in developing countries, provided that the cost has been made affordable. A manufacturer can easily make the same amount of profit – if not more – by selling more numbers in developing countries at a lower cost than by selling less numbers at a higher cost in developed countries. For instance, in the case of screen reading software for mobile phones, the cost was brought down to less than one-fourth by just projecting a higher volume of sales. The Saksham Trust (charitable registered not-for-profit trust in India promoting affordable software) was able to negotiate with the company selling such software in large quantities, which ended up benefiting a lot more users that we could have with the original price per unit.

Policies and legal provisions can play a big role in this issue. For instance, making accessibility compulsory for public information systems or workplaces would ensure much larger procurement of technology products. This would, in turn, bring costs down considerably, as well as allow for further development of such technologies in developing countries.

UN Agencies have an important role to play in the formation of appropriate policies and laws related to social issues within a given country. For instance, the "United Nations Decade of Disabled Persons, 1983-1992", led to an initiative of UNESCAP (United Nations Economic and Social Commission for Asia and the Pacific), which resulted in the enactment of laws for the protection of the rights of persons with disabilities in many of the countries in the Asia-Pacific region. The Indian law for the protection of the rights of persons with disabilities enacted in 1995 is one such example.

However, although this law makes provisions for an accessible physical environment, it does not specify whether accessibility extends to ICTs. The implications of such laws for ICTs need to be made clear. Another avenue to achieve such result will be to translate the Convention on the Rights of Persons with Disabilities into the national laws of each ratifying Member State.

Another good example is the DAISY for All Project (DFA), which is being implemented by the DAISY Consortium and of which I am the Assistant Project Manager. Through the DAISY for All Project, focal points for creation and distribution of accessible digital content are being established in developing countries. The project not only provides basic infrastructure for establishing such focal points, but also providing several levels of training to develop human resources who are equipped with the latest technology and knowledge about ICT accessibility. The project is building networks among disability organizations, engineering universities, government education and social welfare departments in beneficiary countries.

Establishment of these focal points has resulted in the formation of the DAISY Lanka Foundation in Sri Lanka, the DAISY Forum of Pakistan, the DAISY Forum of India, and the Nepal DAISY foundation, to name a few. Wide participation in these forums has not only helped establish services, such as talking book libraries, but has also created awareness in government and non-government agencies about ICT Accessibility issues. Concerted efforts are thus being made to create policies for content accessibility in developing countries.

The DFA Project is also developing software for the authoring and playback of accessible multimedia content, which is helpful in creating and reading books that are universally accessible to populations with and without disabilities. This multimedia content-creating system is also capable of developing accessible disaster warning systems and awareness campaigns for issues like HIV/AIDS to all sectors of a given population, including those who are illiterate or those, such as Aborigines, who do not have any written script for their language. The software being developed under the DFA project is open source and thus easily adaptable to local languages, regardless of whether or not text-to-speech is involved. For instance, AMIS (Audio Messaging Interchange Specification), a software used for playback of multimedia content is already available in more than 12 languages of developing countries.

We need to ensure the development of basic technologies, such as text-to-speech engines or OCR (Optical Character Recognition) software, that adhere to international API (Application Programming Interface) standards and that can be easily adapted to local languages of developing countries. It is equally important to enact policies and laws for ensuring accessibility of ICT infrastructures that are installed on a large scale in developing countries. Furthermore, policies must be implemented to cut down costs that end-users currently incur in order to access technology. In order to achieve the above objectives, dissemination of good practices across various sectors and regions is essential.

South Africa: Parliamentary Life and Accessibility

By Hendrietta Ipeleng Bogopane-Zulu
Member of the South African Parliament, National Assembly,
Chairperson of the South African Delegation to the Preparatory
Commission of the Convention on the Rights of Persons with
Disabilities

Amongst the yardsticks by which to measure a society's respect for human rights, to evaluate it's level of maturity and generosity of spirit is done by looking at the state's benefits to those who have less in society and who are most vulnerable: senior citizens, persons with disabilities, and children.

It is not my intent to cover much parliamentary jargon, except to say that, in the area of ICT, the South Africa Parliament – as the only parliament in the world having 20 of its members with varying disabilities – would make an excellent partner in the accessibility movement. The members with disabilities bring with them a lot of talent with regards to the management of Parliament – and also with regards to politics in South Africa at large. It is important for me to indicate that the large number of parliamentary members with disabilities in South Africa has nothing to do with a quota, but is rather a pure function of merit. That is not to say, however, that integrating persons with disabilities into Parliament has been an easy task. For example, given that one our members of Parliament is deaf, the issue arose as to where the sign language interpreter would sit and whether or not he would have to take an oath. There were other realities of accessibility that existed in terms of engaging with other members of the Parliament. For instance, how could a deaf member be expected to yell over the others to be heard (which was a standard parliamentary practice)? It was soon decided that ICT-based solutions were the most appropriate for such problems. We took a first step by using flashing lights to call the attention of deaf persons when it is time to begin a parliamentary session. Telephones with blinking lights were also introduced around the Parliament and its various centers.

ICT-based solutions were equally needed for written communication among members of parliament. Much of parliamentary business relies on significant reading, either to prepare for meetings or simply to facilitate communication between members on parliamentary issues. Communication is paper-based; and, as a visually impaired person, I found the roadblocks of such a system to be quite hindering. I needed a large office to be able to store information in Braille format. Furthermore, if correspondence and other materials were in Braille, much more time was needed to read them. Once again, ICTs were needed to solve our functional problems.

The other aspect that I should address is that our Parliament is a very large institution, with some members coming from rural areas with no electricity and no access to motorized wheelchairs. The Parliament was thus faced with the issue of assuring that members could arrive on time at a meeting on one end of the Parliament Building after a meeting at the other end. Once this problem was recognized, the question then became one of access, availability, and affordability of the ICT solutions needed to resolve the issue. The biggest question regarded where we would obtain specialized computers. Furthermore, whenever technology changed, we worried if it was compatible with our accessibility programs. Every time Parliament introduces a new system, we must ask if it is compatible with JAWS, because half of the time it is not.

Another key aspect to consider with regards to assuring accessibility within parliament concerns training. Having gone from attending a school for the blind in a rural area with no electricity to sitting in Parliament, I naturally did not know how to use a computer. Luckily, I was always very interested in computers and made it a priority to learn to use them on my own. There are, however, two other members of parliament with visual impairments, who had never worked with computers. In order to do research to prepare our speeches, we need to be able to access the Internet. Because of affordability issues, we were asked to choose between a "talking computer" or a "human being." What is meant by "human being" is essentially someone from industry who is needed to make the various ICT-based systems within Parliament accessible (e.g. conversion and importation processes).

We have to make sure that, in the process of all of these ICT transformations, we do not create the notion that ICT can replace human touch – because it cannot. Unfortunately, the talking computer cannot walk someone from one meeting room to another. Initially, the dual need for ICT and human assistance was not easy for our presiding officers to understand.

I hope as the global accessibility movement grows and forges new strategic partnerships that the notion of legislation as the be-all and end-all will not be created. Much of the time, it is quite easy –

especially for UN Member States – to comply with UN treaties and conventions. In doing so, a given Member State is often complying by establishing domestic legislation. However, there is no system in place for the UN to hold its Members States accountable for implementing disability legislation. The truth is, even when parliamentarians have passed appropriate legislation, they often do not allocate resources to such provisions, let alone establish a framework by which to monitor its implementation. As such, for all intents and purpose, they do not even know where that legislation is from the day that they passed it. As we develop new ICT solutions, it is important that we not lose sight of this even greater problem on the implementation level.

The main action that industry needs to take with regards to accessibility is to develop goals and standards that take certain realities into consideration. Many of the standards are imposed standards that are very difficult, if not impossible, for developing countries to implement. Therefore, I hope that developing countries can become involved from the very beginning in a number of accessibility initiatives so that standards that take the realities of developing countries into account can be developed and then implemented. If such were the case, a lot more could be done to create legislation to promote equal access to ICTs.

Furthermore, I hope that industry will begin to network more with organizations representing persons with disabilities. In South Africa, we have used our buying power as persons with disabilities to ensure that industry listens to us. One example is the International Day for Persons with Disabilities where we engaged with South Africa's three mobile network providers: Cell C, Vodacom, and MTN. We asked each of the companies if it was prepared to engage in work with us in developing accessible cell phones and related applications. None of the companies took us seriously until we made it clear to them that whichever company was ready to work with us would be receiving business from all of our families and associates. Vodacom was the first company to actually say, "Let's engage with persons with disabilities and you can become our consultant in ensuring that we identify your special needs." Now, Vodacom is one of the most successful providers thanks to their embracing of accessibility. As promised, we created a level of awareness within our own networks and organizations that led to a significant number of customers making the change to Vodacom.

When it comes to issues surrounding procurement, I think that it is the government's responsibility to create an enabling environment by developing preferential procurement policies for those companies who respect accessibility. As accessibility standards are being developed, it is very important for industry to also ensure that persons with disabilities are considered – especially those in developing countries. Moreover, persons with disabilities must be trained and subsequently hired as designers and programmers.

What is most important to keep in mind is that the greater our diversity, the richer our capacity to create new vision. The acknowledgement of our differences and the need to celebrate them must be viewed as capacities rather than as deficiencies. It may be painful, but this inquiry can be the beginning of a new personal future.

An Overview of the Ratification and Implementation Process of the Convention on the Rights of Persons with Disabilities

By Ambassador Anda Filip
Director, Inter-parliamentary Union

The Convention and its Optional Protocol have little value for a State until its government signs, ratifies or accedes to them. States can choose to join the Convention without signing the Optional Protocol. For the Convention to enter into force – that is, to become an instrument of international law – at least twenty States must have joined it by expressing their "consent to be bound" via ratification or accession. For the Optional Protocol, only ten ratifications are required.

Signing the Convention, the first step towards ratification, is usually carried out by a government's Head of State or by a duly appointed representative within the United Nations Secretariat (Treaty Section, Office of Legal Affairs etc.). There is no deadline for signatures and signing the Convention does not create any binding obligations to signing member States. Signature is, nevertheless, an important indication that the signing State will eventually consider ratification. To this end, inherent in signing the treaty is an obligation to refrain from undertaking any action that constitutes an evident violation of the Convention.

Ratification is the second step in the process toward implementation of the Convention. It occurs at two levels: national and international. Nationally, the ratification process varies from State to State, depending on the constitutional structure of the State at hand (e.g. common law vs. civil law tradition). In most cases, Parliament must be involved by enacting a resolution or a bill in support of the ratification. Internationally, ratification occurs when a government communicates its intention to ratify the Convention to the United Nations Secretary-General by depositing the "instrument of ratification." Such an instrument can take any form but would have to consist, at a minimum, of a document signed by the Head of State or Government conveying in clear terms the wish of the State to become a Party to the Convention. It is only when such an instrument is deposited that a State becomes legally bound to the Convention.

Finally, a State can choose to join the Convention by process of accession. This is essentially a shortcut whereby a State simply deposits an "instrument of accession" with the United Nations Secretary-General.

Furthermore, the Convention allows for ratifications to occur "with reservations", a process by which a State is allowed to ratify the Convention or its Optional Protocol even when the country does not agree with specific provisions of the Convention. In most cases, a State will agree with the overall framework and most provisions of the Convention. To this effect, reservations are essentially declarations that a State makes to the effect that it will not consider itself bound by certain provisions of the Convention. Such statements can be made upon signing the Convention, ratification, or accession. Furthermore, reservations are not binding and can be lifted at any time in the event that a State works through the original difficulty posed by the provision(s) in question.

Aside from the formal process of ratification of the Convention, Parliament has a tremendous role to play in its implementation afterwards. In fact, it would be rare for a country to already have legislation in place that completely conforms to every provision outlined in the Convention. The question therefore is how the Convention translates into national law. There are several possibilities, including the following main two: enacting a single law that sanctions the Convention in its entirety as equivalent to national law (except in those countries where the Constitution makes this process automatic) and adopting individual pieces of legislation that implement one or more provisions of the Convention at a time until the whole Convention is implemented.

A good step to consider as a matter of priority is for a new State Party to amend the Constitution or other fundamental law to add a strong anti-discrimination clause to protect the rights of persons with disabilities. Another important step would consist in a systematic review of all existing laws to make sure that such legislation is not in violation of the Convention – and then to enact the required amendments accordingly.

Regardless of the mechanisms by which implementation takes place, it should be anticipated from the beginning as a long term process that may take several years to complete. Signatory States should also be prepared to implement the Convention at the legislative level, as well as through concrete policies on the ground. Most importantly, it should be accepted from the outset that, as was the case during the writing of the Convention itself, persons with disabilities should be intimately involved as principal stakeholders[26] in all legislative and policy-making processes involved in the implementation of the Convention.

---

[26] A comprehensive discussion of the ratification process of the Convention and of its implementation can be found in *From Exclusion to Equality: Realizing the Rights of Persons with Disabilities,* Handbook for Parliamentarians on the Convention on the Rights of Persons with Disabilities and Its Optional Protocol, published by the United Nations, the Office of the United Nations High Commissioner for Human Rights, and the Inter-Parliamentary Union, New York/Geneva 2007.

Best Practices Compendium: A Resource Guide to Accessible and Assistive ICT Applications

This chapter draws on the Global Initiative for Inclusive Information and Communication Technologies' homegrown country profile database to present some of the most compelling case studies from around the world in the realm of ICT solutions for persons living with disabilities. Hand-picked by G3ict staff members, the following case studies span from the most developed to the least developed regions of the world and serve to provide a broad overview of what activities are currently taking place in the realm of assistive technologies.

A live version of this section can be consulted at www.g3ict.com

Synopsis of Case Studies

Case Studies	Africa	Asia	Australia	Europe	North America	South America	Cognitive	Hearing	Lower Mobility	Multiple	Speech	Upper Mobility	Visual	Accessible Appliances	Cellular Telephony	Computer Interface	Geographic Positioning	Integrated Technologies	Public Access Device	Rehabilitation, Therapy	Website	Wireless Application	Education	Employability	Health	Public Access	Safety	Wheelchair Accessory
	Geographic Area						Type of Disability							Type of Technology									Application Area					
AABAC			✓							✓			✓					✓					✓	✓	✓	✓	✓	✓
Access Abill		✓											✓			✓	✓								✓			
Access Israel	✓											✓		✓				✓							✓			
Adaptive Multiple Information System	✓												✓			✓							✓		✓			
Adaptive Technology Center for the Blind	✓												✓			✓								✓				
Archimedes				✓								✓		✓											✓			
ASK-IT			✓							✓						✓	✓								✓			
Assistive Robotic Service Manipulator			✓							✓		✓								✓								✓
Bath Institute of Medical Engineering			✓							✓										✓								✓
BlueEar			✓					✓													✓		✓		✓			
blueIRIS			✓										✓								✓	✓			✓			
Bobby			✓							✓								✓							✓			
Breaking Down Barriers	✓		✓							✓																		
DAISY			✓										✓			✓							✓		✓			
Deaf Alerter			✓					✓											✓			✓					✓	
Deafblind			✓			✓		✓					✓			✓									✓			
DIADEM			✓		✓		✓																✓					
Disabilityart.com		✓								✓											✓				✓			
EZ Access		✓								✓				✓							✓				✓			
Full Access Through Technology				✓				✓						✓											✓			
GameON!			✓							✓							✓			✓					✓			
House of Windows	✓									✓		✓		✓											✓			
MATILDAH																												
Mobile Care			✓					✓				✓		✓														
Mugunghwa Electronics	✓						✓	✓	✓	✓	✓	✓	✓											✓				
Nat'l Accessibility Portal - South Africa	✓									✓			✓													✓		
Neater Eater			✓						✓									✓						✓				
PEBBLES				✓						✓								✓					✓					
PEN-International	✓			✓				✓															✓	✓	✓	✓	✓	✓
POETA					✓					✓								✓					✓	✓				
RoboBraille			✓										✓			✓									✓			
Royal Nat'l Institute for the Blind			✓										✓	✓														
Sightsavers Dolphin Pen	✓												✓	✓		✓							✓	✓				
Stimulation and Therapeutic Activity Ctr	✓									✓													✓					
Talking Tins			✓										✓						✓							✓	✓	
T-Base Communications with Vision		✓											✓	✓											✓			
The Signing Web Project				✓				✓										✓							✓			
Trekker				✓									✓				✓	✓						✓			✓	
Trinity College of Music			✓										✓			✓							✓					
Wheelchairnet.org				✓						✓											✓				✓			
wiseDX			✓									✓				✓		✓										✓
WWAAC				✓						✓								✓							✓			

AABAC

Geographic Area: Europe
Type of Disability: Upper Mobility, Lower Mobility
Type of Technology: Computer Interface
Type of Area of Application: All
Location: United Kingdom

Abstract:
AABAC, an acronym for Adaptive Asynchronous Brain-Actuated Control, is a project currently underway between Essex University and Oxford University. Begun in April of 2006, the project will continue through the end of March 2009. The project aims to develop a novel adaptive and asynchronous brain-computer interface (BCI) system for brain-actuated control of intelligent systems and robots. A BCI system detects and analyses brainwaves in order to understand a user's mental state and then translates the mental states into commands for communicating with and controlling computers, robots, and other systems. AABAC will use adaptive learning to increase the number of control commands mapped from a limited number of mental states. The methods will be assessed using real-time brain-actuated control of an intelligent wheelchair and a robotic arm. BCIs have repaired damaged sight and provided new functionality to paralyzed persons. The AABAC program would allow, for example, those with physical disabilities (with an implanted BCI in their brains) to be able to control computers or robotic limbs simply by thinking about these endeavors.

Website: http://cswww.essex.ac.uk/Research/BCIs/AABAC.html
Contact Person: Dr. John Gan
Contact Telephone: (+44) (0)1206 872770

AccessAbill
Geographic Area: Australia
Type of Disability: Visual
Type of Technology: Computer Interface, Communications
Type of Area of Application: Public Access
Location: Australia

Abstract:
In May of 2007, T-Base Communications, based in Ottowa, Ontario, announced a partnership with Vision Australia to enable those persons in Australia and New Zealand who are blind or have low vision to access financial, telecom, and utility statements – as well as other private and personal information – in Braille, large print, e-text, and audio formats. This unique electronic system designed by T-Base Communications is known as AccessAbill, which sends invoices and statements directly to the consumer in the format of choice. T-Base Communications also works with companies such as American Express, Citigroup, First Data, LaSalle Bank, Merrill Lynch, Nokia, Royal Bank, Symcor, TD, and Verizon Wireless. Formed in 2004, Vision Australia is committed to delivering exceptional and efficient services to the blind and low-vision communities of Australia and New Zealand.

Website: www.tbase.com www.visionaustralia.org.au
Contact Person: Meagan Denyer
Contact Telephone: +61 2 9334 3308
Contact E-mail: megan.denyer@visionaustralia.org

Access Israel

Geographic Area: Middle East/Africa
Type of Disability: Multiple
Type of Technology: Integrated Technologies; Accessible appliances
Type of Area of Application: Public Access
Location: Israel

Abstract:
Access Israel is a non-profit organization dedicated to making Israel accessible to all its citizens and visitors. The organization runs a website providing users with free information about accessible tourism in Israel, highlighting general information about Israel, and providing a database of accessible accommodations, transportation, featured itineraries, and general trip-planning assistance for persons with an array of disabilities.

The organization also spreads awareness to the public and to policy-makers about the importance of accessibility and the potential that citizens with disabilities have to impact society. The organization recognizes the enormous human and business value in the 600,000 persons with disabilities living in Israel and addresses the issue not with pity or dependence, but rather with recognition of the vast potential that can be reached by incorporating persons with disabilities in to all walks of life.

In addition to a website on accessible tourism, Access Israel also works with e-accessibility, provides employment for persons with disabilities, offers web-based accessibility training, lobbies for greater accessibility throughout the state, and raises general accessibility awareness throughout Israel.

Website: www.aisrael.org
Contact Telephone: (+972) 57-239239
Contact Email: hadar@aisrael.org

Adaptive Multiple Information System
Geographic Area: Asia
Type of Disability: Visual
Type of Technology: Computer Interface
Type of Area of Application: Public Access; Education
Location: Japan

Abstract:
AMIS, the Adaptive Multimedia Information System, is an open source initiative hosted by the Japanese Society for Rehabilitation of Persons with Disabilities. In collaboration with the DAISY for All Project and individuals across the world, AMIS gives users an open source software product that provides a flexible user interface for reading DAISY content. As part of the DAISY for All Project, whose goal it is to bring DAISY talking book technology to persons with disabilities in developing countries, AMIS facilitates the provision of playback software in local languages and addresses multiple disabilities by offering a variety of ways to interact with a DAISY publication. Modular AMIS features, such as skins and plug-ins, allow the interface to accommodate a range of needs. Skins define the on-screen interface (visual, textual, and auditory), and plug-ins allow the software to communicate with external devices (e.g., joysticks and Braille displays).

All software is provided free of charge and is available for download from the AMIS website.

Website: www.amisproject.org
Contact Person: Marisa Demeglio, Project Coordinator
Contact Email: marisademeglio@users.sourceforge.net
General Email: info@amisproject.org
Related Links: The Urakawa Project: http://urakawa.sf.net/
The DAISY for All Project: http://www.daisy-for-all.org/
The DAISY Consortium: http://www.daisy.org/
Version 1x of AMIS: http://www.amisproject.org/website/index.html

Adaptive Technology Center for the Blind
Geographic Area: Africa
Type of Disability: Visual
Type of Technology: Computer Interface
Type of Area of Application: Employability
Location: Addis Ababa, Ethiopia

Abstract:
The Adaptive Technology Center for the Blind (ATCB) in Ethiopia is a NGO sponsored by the United Nations Educational, Scientific, and Cultural Organization (UNESCO), developed in 2001 to address the needs of the 500,000 blind and visually impaired individuals in Ethiopia. The purpose of the organization is to use adaptive technology with ICTs to help the visually impaired participate to their fullest potential in society. The ATCB is dedicated to making adaptive technology available to Ethiopian society, thereby replacing old, tedious, and inefficient Braille transcription technologies that often leave visually impaired individuals without access to a large amount of information.

In 2003, the ATCB partnered with UNESCO to create a computer training center for blind users in Ethiopia. ATCB now trains visually impaired citizens in the use of various ICT solutions, giving them the necessary access and skills to compete equally and to provide financially for themselves and for their families.

ATCB is also a public awareness initiative, challenging age-old beliefs and unfavorable social attitudes towards the visually impaired in Ethiopia – a set of ideas that has historically marginalized those with disabilities. The partnership between ATCB and UNESCO will also be launching a training program to create employment opportunities for visually impaired individuals through ICTs.

Website: www.atcb.org (under construction at time of publication)
Contact Person: Gunther Cyranek
Contact Email: gcyranek@unesco.org

Archimedes
Geographic Area: North America
Type of Disability: Multiple
Type of Technology: Accessible appliances
Type of Area of Application: Public Access
Location: Hawaii (University of)

Abstract:
The Archimedes Project was founded in 1992 at Stanford University, relocating to the University of Hawaii in 2003. The project's goal is to ensure that all people are able to fully participate in the global information society, regardless of individual needs, abilities, preferences and culture. The project works to address the inequalities that those with disabilities face by making information appliances accessible. In 1997, the project's Total Access System was recognized as one of the top five innovations in computer engineering and electronics. The system in question can provide access to computers and other electronic devices via speech recognition, head and eye tracking, and other "human-centered interfaces", enabling those with physical disabilities to have access to these technologies in the same ways as able-bodied persons do.

Website: http://archimedes.hawaii.edu/
Contact Person: Neil Scott, Director
Contact Telephone: (+1) 808-842-9857
Contact Email: ngscott@hawaii.edu

Related Links:
Former Archimedes Project at Stanford:
http://archimedes.stanford.edu/
Total Access System Press Releases:
http://archimedes.stanford.edu/press.html

ASK-IT
Geographic Area: Europe
Type of Disability: Multiple
Type of Technology: Cellular Telephony, Integrated Technologies
Type of Area of Application: Public Access
Location: Greece

Abstract:
ASK-IT is an integrated project, partly funded by the European Commission under the 6th Framework Program, e-Inclusion. The driving vision behind the project is to create a service using ICTs to help improve the everyday lives and independence of mobility-challenged individuals in European cities.

The service connects to the individual through a mobile device such as a cell phone or PDA, providing them with access to relevant and real-time information – primarily for traveling, but also for transportation, leisure activities, local services, and other everyday necessities that are wheelchair accessible. Furthermore, the device keeps a personal profile on the user, noting his or her preferences and requirements. Everything from preferred mode of transportation to wheelchair turning radius is stored. The ASK-IT system caters to all the needs and conditions of the user and has the ability communicate information in all European languages in written format, spoken format (for visually impaired individuals) and graphic format (for illiterate individuals).

The system is currently being tested in eight different European cities and has thus far yielded exceptional results. The intelligence of the system is second-to-none in helping persons with disabilities find accessible resources and facilities while traveling. The organization currently has links to more than 360,000 individuals with disabilities and is active partners with a number of federations and social organizations that seek to ensure a better quality of life for all.

Website: www.ask-it.org
Contact Person: Dr. Evangelos Bekiaris, Principal Researcher
Contact Telephone: (+30) 2310-498.265
Contact Email: abek@certh.gr

Assistive Robot Service Manipulator
Geographic Area: Europe
Type of Disability: Lower Mobility; Upper Mobility
Type of Technology: Rehabilitation and Therapy
Type of Area of Application: Wheelchair Accessory
Location: Netherlands

Abstract:
Exact Dynamics is a Dutch firm which has built the Assistive Robot Service Manipulator (ARM) known as "Manus" – a robot which assists persons with severe handicaps in their upper limbs, compensating for lost arm and hand function. Mounted on an electric wheelchair (or any mobile base), it allows for a number of daily living tasks to be carried out through the use of an input device, such as a keypad, 4x4 buttons, a joystick, or any other device attached to a non-disabled body part. The ARM can aid with eating and drinking, taking medicines, preparing meals, using appliances, scratching itches, shaving, brushing teeth, doing the dishes, using light switches, operating a TV or DVD player, turning the pages of books, picking up objects, shopping, opening doors etc. When not in use, the ARM can be folded down beside the wheelchair. The goal of the ARM is to help users with upper limb disabilities to become more self-supportive and participatory in society, thereby increasing their overall quality of life.

Website: http://www.exactdynamics.nl/
Contact Person: Mr. Tim Jones, Engineer
Contact Telephone: +(31) 01869 337395
Contact Email: info@exactdynamics.nl

BIME – Bath Institute of Medical Engineering
Geographic Area: Europe
Type of Disability: Lower Mobility
Type of Technology: Rehabilitation and Therapy
Type of Area of Application: Wheelchair Accessory
Location: United Kingdom

Abstract:
BIME, the Bath Institute of Medical Engineering, has pioneered numerous design and development projects in the field of medial and rehabilitation engineering, working with users and medical professionals to solve problems of disability and healthcare with practical technology. "Football Player", one of the Institute's current projects, highlights this type of innovation. After receiving many requests for a device that would allow wheelchair users to play football (soccer) – as there is currently no such product available – BIME hopes to engineer a pioneering product which will allow those who are in wheelchairs to play football (soccer) in their own way. Two prototype devices – one for powered wheelchair users and one for manual wheelchair users – which trap an incoming ball and fire it out again at the push of a button, have already been developed.

Website: http://www.bime.org.uk/
Contact Telephone: (+44) (0)1225 82 4103
Contact Email: info@bime.org.uk

BlueEar
Geographic Area: Europe
Type of Disability: Hearing
Type of Technology: Wireless Application; Public Access Device
Type of Area of Application: Public Access
Location: Stockholm, Sweden

Abstract:
BlueEar, part of the Bluetooth Assistive Listening System, aims to develop an open system for assistive listening devices based on the new industry radio standard known as "Bluetooth" (digital wireless communication). BlueEar envisions that, in ten years' time, persons will be able to switch their hearing aid to a common channel and pick up sound. The project runs in two parts: first, an investigation of the end-user needs of hard-of-hearing persons, and second, the demonstration of the technical viability of using Bluetooth for assistive listening devices. The first part of the project has already been completed with the production of BlueEar prototypes. Ties to the hearing aid industry have also already been made.

Contact Person: Mr. Ragnar Åhgren
Contact Telephone: (+46) 8-6930900

BlueIRIS
Geographic Area: Europe
Type of Disability: Visual
Type of Technology: Daily Life; Public Access Devices
Type of Area of Application: Public Access
Location: Warrington, England

Abstract:
The Blackpool, Fylde, and Wyre Society for the Blind recently launched a service called blueIRIS using broadband internet to create a radio service for the blind that is available over the Internet. Previously, the Society distributed cassette recordings of daily news from local and international newspapers to blind and visually impaired citizens. The new service, on the other hand, includes the use of computers, broadband Internet, and special software which reads any screen text to users, offers the option of increased text or image size, and eliminates the need for a mouse. blueIRIS provides increased accessibility for users with disabilities by giving them the opportunity to pick and choose what they listen to, as well as by providing access to a greater amount of news content than what was previously available with the recorded cassettes. The software is also being used to help the visually impaired to navigate the Internet.

Website: http://www.blueiris.org.uk/
Contact Email: enquiries@blueiris.info
Related Links: http://www.sustainit.org/case-studies/docs/99-13Blue_Iris.pdf

Bobby

Geographic Area: North America
Type of Disability: Multiple
Type of Technology: Computer Interface
Type of Area of Application: Public Access
Location: United States

Abstract:
Bobby™ was launched in 1996 to help Web designers throughout the world analyze their sites for accessibility for all Internet users, including those with disabilities. This interactive tool examines web pages to identify potential barriers to access. Bobby offers prioritized suggestions based on the Web Content Accessibility Guidelines provided by the World Wide Web Consortium's Web Access Initiative. With the release of Bobby WorldWide, web designers can now test their sites for compliance with the U.S. Federal Government's Section 508 standards. As web designers use Bobby WorldWide, they learn how to address problems within their own sites and subsequently learn skills to design more accessible sites in the future.

Website: http://www.cast.org/bobby
Contact Telephone: (+1) 781 245-2212
Contact Email: cast@cast.org
Related Links:
Center for Applied Special Technology (creators): http://www.cast.org/
University of Toronto web accessibility checker:
http://checker.atrc.utoronto.ca/index.html

"Breaking Down Barriers" International Film Festival

Geographic Area: Europe; Asia
Type of Disability: Multiple
Type of Technology: N/A
Type of Area of Application: Education
Location: Russia

Abstract:
The "Breaking down Barriers" International Disability Film Festival held in Moscow showcased nearly 100 films from 20 countries around the world. The films ranged from documentaries, animated films, films for children, and long and short films – all concerning the topic of disability. The films competed for awards in 11 different categories. The four-day event also included workshops and discussion groups attended by both persons with disabilities and those without.

Website: http://festival-eng.perspektiva-inva.ru/
Contact Organization: Regional Society of Disabled People "Perspektiva"
Contact Telephone: (+7) (495) 245-68-79, (+7) (499) 242-50-94, and (+7) (495) 363-08-39
Contact Email: festival@perspektiva-inva.ru
Related Links:
http://festival-eng.perspektiva-inva.ru/?16
http://festival-eng.perspektiva-inva.ru/?17

DAISY
Geographic Area: Europe
Type of Disability: Visual
Type of Technology: Computer Interface
Type of Area of Application: Public Access, Education
Location: Geneva, Switzerland

Abstract:
DAISY (Digital Accessible Information System) is an open international standard for accessible multimedia. The DAISY Consortium is based in Switzerland, and is made up of leading non-profit organizations from around the world serving blind and dyslexic people. DAISY helps bridge the digital divide in developing regions of the world by ensuring access to information for those who have previously had severely limited or no access to information, such as persons with print disabilities, speakers of minority languages, indigenous populations without a written language, and those who are illiterate. DAISY for All (DFA) is a project to deploy DAISY technology, address goals and objectives (which include capacity building in developing countries), and serve as a catalyst to generate broader alliances that support the global sharing of human knowledge in the information society. DAISY for All is funded by the Nippon Foundation as a five-year project.

Website: http://www.daisy-for-all.org/
Contact Email: Go to http://www.daisy.org/support/contactus.asp, and select "Project: DAISY for All (DFA)" as the message category
Related Links:
Nippon Foundation: http://www.nippon-foundation.or.jp/eng/
The DAISY Consortium: http://www.daisy.org/

Deaf Alerter

Geographic Area: Europe
Type of Disability: Hearing
Type of Technology: Wireless Application; Integrated Technologies
Type of Area of Application: Safety
Location: United Kingdom

Abstract:
Deaf Alerter is a radio-based fire alarm warning and public address messaging system for the deaf and hearing-impaired. The device is capable of both visual (strobe) and physical (vibration pad) warnings. Today, the Deaf Alerter is widely installed in the UK and is now being installed worldwide. The device works as follows: upon seeing the Deaf Alerter sign, a hearing-impaired person knows that the building is equipped with a Deaf Alerter transmitter and that his or her own Alerter (or one borrowed from the building's reception desk) will operate anywhere within that building. While used primarily for fire alarms and public address messaging, it can also be used for bomb evacuations, paging, or an equipment alarm warning. The vibration pad (termed "Night Cradle") is part of the system and provides wake-up features for deaf persons who might be in bed asleep at the time of an emergency.

Website: http://www.deaf-alerter.com/website.htm
Contact Telephone: (+44) (0)1332 363981
Contact Email: info@deaf-alerter.com

Deafblind

Geographic Area: Europe
Type of Disability: Hearing, Visual
Type of Technology: Computer Interface
Type of Area of Application: Public Access
Location: United Kingdom

Abstract:
Deafblind is a website offering free software for persons who are deaf-blind or have learning disabilities to help them to pursue more knowledge, explore their surroundings, and become more independent. The project was established by Sense and the University of Manchester. Furthermore, Sense has three ICT centers in the UK for deaf-blind citizens where the software is used. Deafblind is currently looking at ways to attract a wider audience to its website.

Website: http://www.deafblindonline.co.uk/
Contact Person: Ms. Samantha Denyer
Contact Telephone: (+44) (0)20 7272 7774

DIADEM
Geographic Area: Europe
Type of Disability: Cognitive
Type of Technology: Multiple
Type of Area of Application: Education
Location: European Union

Abstract:
DIADEM, or Delivering Inclusive Access for Disabled or Elderly Members of the community, is an EU funded project coordinated by Brunel University (UK) to develop next-generation assistive systems that empower persons with disabilities (and aging citizens) to play a full role in society by increasing their autonomy and helping them to realize their maximum potential. With the help of partners such as the Norwegian National Computer Center, Bluegarden (Norway), MORE (Norway), and CSI Piemonte (Italy), the project will provide greater dialogue to counteract the issues faced by many users with cognitive disabilities. For example, persons with cognitive disabilities can suffer from poor concentration and loss of short-term memory, which means that they are more likely to lose track of where they are in a particular process or get lost in an online transaction. In addition, reduced problem solving skills and loss of mental flexibility mean that users are more likely to become frustrated by requests for input that are unexpected, irrelevant, or appear out of sequence. To this end, DIADEM aims to provide support to help these users. The project received 1.95 million euros from the European Union, and is set to run from September 1, 2006 to August 31, 2009.

Website: http://www.project-diadem.eu/
Contact Person: Dr. Tony Elliman, Project Coordinator
Contact Telephone: (+44) 1895 266022
Contact Email: tony.elliman@brunel.ac.uk
General Information: info@project-diadem.eu

Disabilityart.com
Geographic Area: North America
Type of Disability: Multiple
Type of Technology: Website
Type of Area of Application: Education
Location: Florida, USA

Abstract:
Disablityart.com is a website which creates and compiles positive images of persons with disabilities in everyday-life situations and inclusive settings. The site facilitates the purchase of the images in collections in CD-Rom format or on a by-image basis. The images can be used to communicate the work of an organization (as is the case with other groups, such as Wheelchairnet), whether that be on brochures, in existing publications, on web pages, or in training and educational materials. In essence, the site facilitates the transfer of information through dynamic visual expressions, thereby raising awareness of different types of disabilities and offering an effective educational tool.

Website: www.disabilityart.com
Contact Email:info@disabilityart.com
Related Links:
Australian counter-part:
http://www.spectronicsinoz.com/product.asp?product=432

EZ Access

Geographic Area: North America
Type of Disability: Multiple
Type of Technology: Cellular Telephony; Public Access Devices
Type of Area of Application: Public Access
Location: Wisconsin (University of)

Abstract:
EZ Access® is a simple set of interface enhancements which can be applied to existing electronic products and devices to increase accessibility. EZ Access enhancements can be applied to a wide range of interactive electronic systems – from public information and transaction machines, such as kiosks, to personal handheld devices like cellular phones. By using EZ Access, developers can create products and devices that are more usable in a wider range of environments and contexts. The blue diamond EZ Help button only appears on devices that have approved implementations of access features and techniques belonging to the EZ Access system.

Website: http://trace.wisc.edu/projects/ez/
Contact Telephone: Trace Research & Development Center: (+1) 608 262-6966
Contact Email: EZ@trace.wisc.edu

Full Access through Technology
Geographic Area: Europe
Type of Disability: Hearing
Type of Technology: Cellular Telephony
Type of Area of Application: Public Access
Location: United Kingdom

Abstract:
FATT, Full Access through Technology, is a program which works to make more effective use of interpreters for the deaf. Since there is just one interpreter per every 140 deaf persons in the United Kingdom, FATT seeks to leverage emerging technology to maximize this finite commodity. The project hopes to set up a system for locating and booking an interpreter that is more than ad-hoc, by establishing an emergency call-out system and central administration. By using a bespoke database and a messaging system, a uniform method of booking is possible. The project is being carried out by Just Communication.

Website: http://www.justcommunication.com/
Contact Person: Mr. Richard Weaver
Contact Telephone: (+44) (0)1527 582080
Contact Email: office@justcommunication.co.uk

GameON!

Geographic Area: Europe
Type of Disability: Multiple
Type of Technology: Computer Interface, Rehabilitation, and Therapy
Location: Oxford, England

Abstract:
The British-based Ace Center Advisory Trust has developed a program called GameON!, which gives children with disabilities the ability to play computer and video games in the same way that their friends without disabilities do. GameON! provides accessibility information on games, adapts them for use by children with disabilities, and offers support and information about parallel technologies, such as joysticks, rollerballs, speech recognition software, etc. The principal issue with the gaming software that is currently on the market is that, before purchase, insufficient information is available about the level of the game's accessibility. As such, many consumers are forced to buy the game, only to subsequently realize that it is missing functions necessary for use by a child with a disability. GameON!'s service is centered around a website which contains a huge database of accessibility information on pre-existing games and numerous downloadable games specifically formatted for use by children with certain disabilities, as well as reviews of games and devices written by the GameON! team and by the users themselves. GameON! was designed as a three-year initiative (from 2004-2007) and remains active thanks to donations from individuals and organizations.

Website: http://www.gameonbeta.org.uk/
Contact Person: Special Effect (owner company)
Contact Telephone: (+44) (0)1608 811909 or (+44) (0)791 807 7177
Contact Email: info@specialeffect.org.uk

House of Windows
Geographic Area: Asia
Type of Disability: Multiple
Type of Technology: Computer Interface
Type of Area of Application: Public Access
Location: Israel

Abstract:
Historically, being a person with a disability in Israel has meant extremely limited access to accessible technology, including access to Internet-based resources. In 2004, Microsoft launched the "House of Windows" program in Israel to make existing community technology centers (CTCs) accessible for persons with disabilities. The program outfits these existing centers with the technology (i.e. special hardware to promote comfort, software for those with visual or hearing disabilities, etc.), and computer and Internet training programs which provide individuals with disabilities access to technology that had previously never been available to them.

Open to the public and serving individuals with a wide range of disabilities – from autism to physical and age-induced handicaps – the centers have provided hundreds of citizens with the skills and knowledge to participate effectively in modern society. Currently in five CTCs throughout the country, Microsoft provides funding and software while partnering with Access Israel and the Israel Association of Community Centers to aid the estimated 13% of the population with disabilities.

Website:
http://www.microsoft.com/about/corporatecitizenship/citizenship/giving/programs/up/casestudies/housewindows.mspx
Contact Telephone: +(972) 57-239239
Contact Email: hadar@aisrael.org
Related Links:
http://www.aisrael.org/Eng/Index.asp?CategoryID=31&ArticleID=56&SearchParam=House%20of%20Windows

MATILDAH

Geographic Area: Europe
Type of Disability: Multiple
Type of Technology: Integrated Technologies
Type of Area of Application:
Location: United Kingdom

Abstract:
MATILDAH, or Making Advanced Technology Useful for Independent Living for Disabled People at Home, brings technology developers and persons with disabilities together in order to develop systems that can be both more effective and more widely-used. The premise of MATILDAH holds that, though there exists a wide range of advanced technology to help persons with disabilities live independently at home, these products and services are designed without the input of persons with disabilities themselves. MATILDAH thus strives to examine the use, role, and application of various ICT-based solutions for those with disabilities in order to make practical recommendations and provide input for future design processes. The project runs from October 23, 2006 until October 22, 2008.

Website: http://www.matildah.org.uk/
Contact Person: Professor Jennifer Harris
Contact Telephone: (+44) (0)1382 464000
Contact Email: info@matildah.org.uk

Mobile Care
Geographic Area: Europe
Type of Disability: Hearing- and Speech
Type of Technology: Cellular Telephony
Type of Area of Application: Public Access
Location: Italy

Abstract:
In a country with more than 1,600,000 deaf-mutes, Telecom Italia teamed up with the cooperation of ENS (National Agency for Deaf-Mutes) to allow the use of cellular phones and mobile telephony services in sign language free of charge. The project, named "Mobile Care", has been in operation since December 2005. Through the project, the user connects to Mobile TV and selects a function. Then, a virtual assistant displayed on the screen of the mobile phone uses Italian Sign Language to provide information concerning the use of mobile phones and relevant services. As a result of Mobile Care, Telecom Italia Mobile (TIM) has improved the accessibility of display panels and services, such as video calls and mobile Internet connection, for the hearing- and speech-impaired.

Website: http://www.telecomitalia.com/
Contact Telephone: (+39) 011 4356503
Contact Email: corporate.affairs@telecomitalia.it

Mugunghwa Electronics

Geographic Area: East Asia
Type of Disability: Multiple
Type of Technology: Electronics
Type of Area of Application: Employment
Location: Suwon, South Korea

Abstract:
In 1994, Samsung Electronics invested over US $23 million to build Mugunghwa Electronics on a 5,875m2 site. This was the first production facility in the country to employ persons with disabilities. 80% of the workers at this facility have either Category 1 or Category 2 disabilities. The operation has remained profitable and was upgraded to subsidiary status in 2002. In 2004, a decade after its establishment, Mugunghwa Electronics' monthly sales reached US $1 million. Mugunghwa Electronics started out as a model case study when it was launched on Disabled Persons Day in 1994.

The operation produces hand-carried vacuum cleaners, mobile phone rechargers, parts for wide-screen TVs, and main boards for DVD players. The vacuum cleaners are exported to the US, Canada, Europe, and China. To heighten the company's technological power, Mugunghwa Electronics also began producing driving equipment for persons with disabilities, together with the Nissan Company in Japan. Furthermore, Mugunghwa Electronics has maintained "sisterhood" ties with Honda Taiyang, established for persons with disabilities by Honda in 1996. The two companies exchange 3-4 workers for two-week intervals to promote cooperation and to benchmark one another.

The company also provides wonderful benefits and facilities to its employees, including on-site residences, sports facilities, a physical therapy center, a karaoke room, and visual arts courses.

Website: http://mugunghwaland.com/eng/
Contact Telephone: +82 31 210 2427
Related Links:
Samsung Electronics Social Contribution Activities:
http://www.samsung.com/AboutSAMSUNG/ELECTRONICSGLOBA
L/SocialCommitment/Greport/03_society/welfare_01.htm

National Accessibility Portal – South Africa
Geographic Area: Africa
Type of Disability: Multiple
Type of Technology: Integrated Technologies; Accessibility
Type of Area of Application: Public Access
Location: South Africa

Abstract:
The National Accessibility Portal (NAP) in South Africa is a five-year initiative aimed at increasing the inclusion of persons with disabilities into mainstream society. The NAP will be a one-stop resource where individuals with a diverse array of disabilities, as well as their caregivers and medical professionals, can seek relevant information, services, and communication specifically focused on the South African community of persons with disabilities.

The NAP provides disability-related information in all South African languages, including information about legislation, available jobs, the use of special equipment, accessibility advice, sports and cultural events, health and rehabilitation issues, medical services and advice, international links, etc. The NAP website provides free online training both on disability products and in the use of ICTs in the workplace. The initiative is also working on the development of new technology solutions to enable persons with disabilities to overcome specific interaction challenges. In addition, the NAP is dedicated to finding statistics related to disabilities and making them available to the government and to the general public, thus enabling new forms of government services, such as improved logistics and the provision of transport to persons with disabilities.

The project's aim is to help government and society overcome the notion that persons with disabilities have no option but to be dependent on welfare. Instead, with the help of enabling ICTs, persons with disabilities can become active and productive members of society.

Website: http://www.napsa.org.za/index.htm
Contact Person: Kagiso Chikane
Contact Telephone: +(27) 012 841 2317
Contact Email: kchikane@csir.co.za

Neater Eater
Geographic Area: Europe
Type of Disability: Lower Mobility
Type of Technology: Integrated Technology
Type of Area of Application: Health
Location: United Kingdom

Abstract:
The Neater Eater was originally a project that began in 1998 and has since evolved in to a product of the same name which is produced commercially and has gone through product versions 2-5 since its initial release. The initial goal of the Neater Easter project was to develop a feeding aid for people with severe tremors, ataxia, or physical disabilities that make independent eating difficult. The project developed an electrically powered apparatus to assist in both eating and drinking. The device allows for full adjustment between individuals, such as the ability for persons to set their own pace for eating and drinking. The latest version can be set for up tofivedifferent users, has an LCD display with multi-language support, and has a plug capability for a joystick. Although the creator of the product was Neater Solutions Ltd., other organizations involved were Chailey Heritage and Business Link.

Website: http://www.neater.co.uk/main.htm
Contact Person: Mr. Jon Michaelis, Managing Director, Neater Solutions Ltd.
Contact Telephone: (+44) (0)1298 23882
Contact Email: E-mail contacts based on country of origin/need: please see http://www.neater.co.uk/main.htm, and go to the "contact" tab
Related Links: Product Website:
http://www.therafin.com/neatereater.htm

PEBBLES – Providing Education by Bringing Learning Environments to Students

Geographic Area: North America
Type of Disability: Multiple
Type of Technology: Computer Interface
Type of Area of Application: Education
Location: Canada

Abstract:
Providing Education by Bringing Learning Environments to Students (PEBBLES) is an innovative system that combines video conferencing technologies with simple robotics technology to allow a student confined to the hospital or to home to attend his or her regular school. PEBBLES places one of its units inside the classroom and its counterpart in the hospital or home of the student. The system allows the student to maintain both a connection to and a presence in his or her normal learning environment. The overarching goal of pebbles is to create a healthier and less stressful environment for a student who is hospitalized or who has a disability.

Website: http://www.ryerson.ca/pebbles/
Contact Person: Bertha Konstantinidis
Contact Telephone: (+1) 416 979-5000 ext. 7620
Contact Email: bkonstan@ryerson.ca

PEN-International

Geographic Area: North America
Type of Disability: Hearing
Type of Technology: Various
Type of Area of Application: Education, Employability
Location: Rochester, New York

Abstract:
Funded by the Nippon Foundations since 2001, the Postsecondary Education Network International (PEN-International) is a project of the National Technical Institute for the Deaf (NTID) to help colleges throughout the world improve technological education for their deaf students. Deaf students attending specific colleges in Japan, China, Russia, the Philippines, Korea, Thailand, Hong Kong, and the Czech Republic have benefited from PEN-International's expertise through improved curriculum, increased access, new technology, multimedia labs, and trained faculty. More recently, PEN-International has been conducting training in the areas of sign language instruction, interpreter training, automation technology, and counseling skills. PEN-International hopes to thus expand career opportunities for deaf and hard-of-hearing students.

Website: http://www.pen.ntid.rit.edu/
Contact Person: James J. DeCaro, Director
Contact Telephone: (+1) 585-475-6319
Contact Email: jjd8074@rit.edu
Related Links:
Nippon Foundation: http://www.nippon-foundation.or.jp/eng/

POETA

Geographic Area: Latin America
Type of Disability: Multiple
Type of Technology: Computer Interface
Type of Area of Application: Education, Employability
Location: Latin America

Abstract:
The Partnership in Opportunities for Employment through Technology in the Americas (POETA) is a joint venture between Microsoft and the Organization of American States (OAS), who partnered in 2001 to work towards technological and educational development in OAS member states. POETA itself began under the Trust for the Americas in 2004 and 2005 and provides technology job retraining and job placement assistance to youth and adults with disabilities at centers located throughout Latin America. POETA benefits approximately 12,500 people directly each year. To date, The Trust for the Americas has thirty-nine operational POETA centers in the following Latin American countries: Argentina, Colombia, Dominican Republic, Ecuador, El Salvador, Guatemala, Honduras, Mexico, Panama, Peru, and Venezuela. The long-term goal of POETA is to establish at least one POETA center in every country in the hemisphere by 2010 and to reach 50,000 people by 2015.

Website: http://www.trustfortheamericas.org/OP%20mail%20eng.pdf
Contact Person: David Rojas, Program Manager
Contact Email: drojas@oas.org

RoboBraille

Geographic Area: Europe
Type of Disability: Visual
Type of Technology: Computer Interface
Type of Area of Application: Public Access
Location: Denmark

Abstract:
RoboBraille is an email-based translation service capable of translating documents to and from contracted Braille and to synthetic speech. The service is available free of charge to all non-commercial users. Users submit documents (e.g., text files, Word documents, HTML pages) as email attachments. The translated results are then returned to the user via email – typically within a matter of minutes. The user can send an e-mail with a document attachment to one of several e-mail accounts used to manage the translation process (e.g., eightdot@robobraille.org for eight-dot Braille translation; sixdot@robobraille.org for six-dot Braille translation). Similarly, localized versions of the e-mail accounts are used to control the language-specific translations, as well as the language of any response sent back to the user. As an example, mail to ottepunkt@robobraille.org will result in Danish eight-dot Braille translation and a user response in Danish, whereas mail to sixdot@robobraille.org will result in English six-dot Braille translation and a user response in English. Additionally, RoboBraille can change text to speech through a similar process which turns a document into an MPE audio file. Users can control the speech rate by inserting plusses or minuses into the subject line of their e-mails, anywhere along the spectrum in which three minuses (---) result in the slowest speech rate and three plusses (+++) result in the fastest speech rate.

Website: http://www1.robobraille.org/websites/acj/robobraille.nsf
Contact Person: Contact varies by country; for a complete list of contacts, please see project website.
Contact Email: Please see link under "contact person" for a full listing of email contacts or email contact@robobraille.org

Royal National Institute for the Blind
Geographic Area: Europe
Type of Disability: Visual
Type of Technology: Accessibility
Location: United Kingdom

Abstract:

The Royal National Institute for the Blind in the United Kingdom has launched an accessibility resource website concerning the accessibility issues related to software. While most websites devoted to accessibility issues concern the accessibility of online data and websites, this initiative provides information, advice, and guidelines for software developers to design software programs that meet the accessibility guidelines being set in the UK.

The "Software Access Center" provides examples of best practices among software designs, as well as advice on how to easily make the program accessible. Furthermore, information on laws, standards, testing, and evaluation are posted in order to give developers a better understanding of the necessities and expectations for software accessibility. The Royal National Institute for the Blind also provides a list of five key recommendations to help observe first-hand how users with disabilities will interact with the program.

Website:
http://www.rnib.org.uk/xpedio/groups/public/documents/PublicWebsite/public_sachome.hcsp
Contact Person: Technology Team
Contact Telephone: (+44) (0) 845 900 0015
Contact Email: ict@rnib.org.uk

Sightsavers Dolphin Pen

Geographic Area: Africa
Type of Disability: Visual
Type of Technology: Computer Interface; Accessible Appliances
Type of Area of Application: Education
Location: Kenya (also worldwide)

Abstract:
Sightsavers International, a NGO based in the UK, is working with the Dolphin Company to provide visually impaired students and individuals in Africa equal access and independence in computer use. The new Sightsavers Dolphin Pen is a small piece of technology providing users with the freedom and flexibility to use any computer without the hassles of finding special software or having to depend on assistance. The product is simple: a pen drive preloaded with a formatted screen reader and magnification software, allowing the user to carry his or her enabling software with him or her for use on any computer.

Partnering with Sightsavers, Dolphin is providing Sightsavers Dolphin Pens to schools all over Africa so that visually impaired students can be educated side-by-side fully-sighted children. Whereas previously there would be approximately one computer for every 30 visually impaired students (drastically slowing their education), now students can use their screen reading software on all computers, giving them equal access to education. In a country plagued by a 45% unemployment rate, giving visually impaired students the ability to learn at the same rate as sighted children secures their prospects, as they enter the job market as adults.

Website:
http://www.sightsavers.net/Press%20Office/Press%20Releases/World4837.html
Contact Person: Nicola Davies
Contact Telephone: +(254) 01444 446733
Contact Email: ndavies@sightsavers.org
Related Links:
http://www.yourdolphin.com/productdetail.asp?id=8

Stimulation and Therapeutic Activity Center
Geographic Area: Asia
Type of Disability: Multiple
Type of Technology: Various
Type of Area of Application: Education
Location: Philippines

Abstract:
The Breaking Barriers for Children project, a partnership between KAMPI, the National Federation of Disabled Persons in the Philippines (Disabled Peoples International-Philippines), and PTU, the Danish Society of Polio and Accident Victims, established the Stimulation and Therapeutic Activity Center (STAC), providing rehabilitation services to over 8,000 children with disabilities in 14 different provinces. In addition to rehabilitation services, the centers provide social services that aim to change negative attitudes toward persons with disabilities within education. The project has also established STAC Satellite Centers in rural villages in order to prevent high transportation costs to families.

Website:
http://www1.worldbank.org/devoutreach/july05/textonly.asp?id=318
Related Links: http://www1.worldbank.org/devoutreach/index.asp

Talking Tins
Geographic Area: Europe
Type of Disability: Visual
Type of Technology: Daily Life
Type of Area of Application: Health, Safety
Location: United Kingdom

Abstract:
"Talking Tins" is a recent project of Talking Products Ltd., which specializes in devices for the visually impaired. Talking Tins helps blind persons determine the contents of canned food, as well as identify other household containers, such as bottles, sprays, and storage containers. The product comes in the form of a magnetic cap that sits on top of any sized tin. The cap allows a person to record a short voice message up to ten seconds, which can then be played back at any time with the touch of a button. It can also be strapped onto other containers. The Talking Tin is reusable, as the voice messages are re-recordable.

Website: http://www.talkingproducts.co.uk/talking_tins.php
Contact Person: Mr. Brian Stickley
Contact Telephone: General: (+44) (0)1794 516677
Contact Email: info@TalkingProducts.com

T-Base Communications with Vision Australia
Geographic Area: Australia
Type of Disability: Visual
Type of Technology: Communications
Type of Area of Application: Public Access
Location: Australia

Abstract:
In May of 2007, T-Base Communications, based in Ottowa, Ontario, announced a partnership with Vision Australia to enable those persons in Australia and New Zealand who are blind or have low vision to access financial, telecom, and utility statements – as well as other private and personal information – in Braille, large print, e-text, and audio formats. This unique electronic system designed by T-Base Communications is known as AccessAbill, which sends invoices and statements directly to the consumer in the format of choice. T-Base Communications also works with companies such as American Express, Citigroup, First Data, LaSalle Bank, Merrill Lynch, Nokia, Royal Bank, Symcor, TD, and Verizon Wireless. Formed in 2004, Vision Australia is committed to delivering exceptional and efficient services to the blind and low-vision communities of Australia and New Zealand.

Websites:
T-Base Communications: www.tbase.com
Vision Australia: www.visionaustralia.org.au
Contact Person:
T-Base Communications: Deanna White, Media and Partner Relations
Vision Australia: Megan Denyer, Public Relations Officer
Contact Telephone:
T-Base Communications: (613) 236-0866 Ext. 231
Vision Australia: (+61) 2 9334 3308 or 1300 84 74 66 (general)
Contact Email:
T-Base Communications: dwhite@tbase.com
Vision Australia: megan.denyer@visionaustralia.org

The Signing Web Project
Geographic Area: North America
Type of Disability: Hearing
Type of Technology: Computer Interface
Type of Area of Application: Public Access
Location: Canada

Abstract:
The Signing Web project is an ongoing initiative of the Adaptive Technology Resource Centre in Canada. It has developed a technique that, for the first time, enables sign language-based websites on the Internet. An authoring tool called SignEd creates the web pages by marking up sign language video files with sign language-based hyperlinks called "signlinks." Users can become members and upload their own signing files.

Website: http://www.aslpah.ca/
Contact Email: info@aslpah.ca

Trekker

Geographic Area: North America
Type of Disability: Visual
Type of Technology: Geographic Positioning; Integrated
Technologies; Wireless Application
Type of Area of Application: Safety
Location: California, USA

Abstract:
Built from a concept originally conceived by the European Space
Association, HumanWare's Trekker is a revolutionary new travel tool
for the blind that uses GPS and talking menus to give directions,
pinpoint user location, and provide real-time information on
surroundings. The Trekker is the first GPS-based product to offer
digital maps to the visually impaired in a fully portable application. The
device is made up of a lightweight pocket PC comfortably worn over
the shoulder on a strap. It announces the names of streets, intersections,
addresses, stores, businesses, restaurants, and area attractions as they
come up. There is also a search function and a "where am I?" key that
can pinpoint one's location. The Trekker even warns of dead ends and
allows the user to take notes through a built-in microphone or Braille
entry, which are then stored for future reference. The Trekker is the
most widely used GPS system for the blind today.

Website:
http://www.humanware.com/en-
usa/products/orientation/gps/_details/id_30/trekker.html
Contact Telephone: (+1) 925 680-7100 and toll-free phone (US only):
(+1) 800 722-3393
Contact Email: us.info@humanware.com
Related Links:
Sendero Group, another creator of portable GPS systems for the blind:
http://www.senderogroup.com/

Trinity College of Music
Geographic Area: Europe
Type of Disability: Visually Impaired
Type of Technology: Computer Interface
Type of Area of Application: Education
Location: Greenwich, London, UK

Abstract:
The Trinity College of Music in the United Kingdom prides itself on providing a music education that is equally accessible for all individuals. Beginning in September 2003, however, the two coinciding software programs being used by visually impaired individuals to read and create music were no longer compatible with PCs. The college was therefore forced to take the classes requiring the use of computer programs out of the core curriculum requirements to ensure equality in grading for all students. Recently, however, Trinity created a program to make Applied Music Technology available to all students, regardless of physical ability. The solution included two modules of the BMus program to teach contemporary recording techniques and to enable composers to engage in acoustic and electro-acoustic composition.

The program set out to work with several visually impaired students of music, most of whom had had little to no experience with computers. Solutions that the college made available to students included the combination of screen-reading software, music notation software using Braille, talking scripts, audio recording software, and CD burning software. The students were walked through the technology and immediately began using it to create and read music at levels that were never available to them previously.

Website:
http://www.bicpa.ac.uk/casestudies/making_music_tech_accessible.ht ml
Contact Person: James Hitchins, Disability Project Officer
Contact Telephone: (+44) (0)20 8305 4418
Contact Email: jhitchins@tcm.ac.uk

Wheelchairnet.org
Geographic Area: North America
Type of Disability: Lower Mobility
Type of Technology: Website
Type of Area of Application: Education
Location: Pittsburgh, USA

Abstract:
Wheelchairnet.org is a comprehensive website which covers all aspects of life for wheelchairs users, including community resources and access to the latest relevant research. Through its virtual community, users can ask or answer questions, share knowledge, link to information about wheelchair products and services, and learn about and participate in wheelchair research projects. The site includes resources for customers, clinicians, case managers, rehabilitation technology suppliers, and insurance companies. Among the most helpful resources for wheelchair users provided by the site are options for wheelchair funding, information on wheelchair industry standards, and links to advocacy and support groups specifically tailored to a person's age, gender, or gravity of disability. In essence, Wheelchairnet.org is a breakthrough virtual community for persons with a common interest in wheelchair technology. The site is free to all users and is sponsored by the RERC (Rehabilitation Engineering Research Center) on Wheeled Mobility at the University of Pittsburgh.

Website: www.wheelchairnet.org
Contact Telephone: (+1) 412-586-6908
Contact Email: ruffing@shrs.pitt.edu

WiseDX

Geographic Area: Europe
Type of Disability: Lower Mobility
Type of Technology: Daily Life; Computer Interface
Type of Area of Application: Wheelchair Accessory
Location: United Kingdom

Abstract:
Originally conceived by the Institute of Child Health at a hospital in London, wiseDX was a project which built a technology of the same name that integrates other assistive technologies, allowing one to drive a powered wheelchair, access a communication aid, and control a computer remotely all in one system. The project's goal was to design a switch system to replace individual controls in the household. The system is available for persons who use one to six switches, combination switches, and switched joysticks. WiseDX is billed as an all-in-one control system for operating wheelchairs and household equipment and is now sold commercially.

Website: http://www.wisedx.com
Contact Person: Colin Clayton
Contact Telephone: (+44) (0)20 7242 9789
Contact Email: info@wisedx.com or see
http://www.wisedx.com/Contacts.htm

WWAAC - World-Wide Augmentative and Alternative Communication Project

Geographic Area: Europe
Type of Disability: Multiple
Type of Technology: Computer Interface
Type of Area of Application: Public Access
Location: United Kingdom

Abstract:
WWAAC, the World-Wide Augmentative and Alternative Communication Project, was a pan-European initiative to make web- and e-mail-based technology more accessible to persons with communication, language, and/or cognitive impairments. The project recognized that, since both the worldwide web and organization-wide intranets require the ability to use text (traditional orthography), virtually none of the major ICT services widely available in society could be used without adaptation. This was especially the case for users with multiple impairments caused by congenital or acquired brain injury, including deficits in: impressive and/or expressive language, motor function (including speech), perception (interpretation and integration of sensory input), concentration and orientation, and memory and general cognitive capacity. One of the most successful outcomes of the project was the development of a web browser and navigation tool that would allow individuals to use symbols to support communication. A free download of the browser can be obtained from the project website.

A further significant innovation was the initial development of a system for ascribing codes to words based on their meanings or concepts. These concept codes can be transmitted between users of different symbol languages and the messages displayed in the symbol language of the choice of the recipient.

Website: http://www.wwaac.eu/
Contact Person: Mr. Andrew Lysley
Contact Telephone: (+44) (0)1865 759800
Related Links: Handicom (a consortium partner)
http://www.handicom.nl/english/Wwaac/index.asp

Appendix

Convention on the Rights of Persons with Disabilities

Preamble

The States Parties to the present Convention,

(a) *Recalling* the principles proclaimed in the Charter of the United Nations which recognize the inherent dignity and worth and the equal and inalienable rights of all members of the human family as the foundation of freedom, justice and peace in the world,

(b) *Recognizing* that the United Nations, in the Universal Declaration of Human Rights and in the International Covenants on Human Rights, has proclaimed and agreed that everyone is entitled to all the rights and freedoms set forth therein, without distinction of any kind,

(c) *Reaffirming* the universality, indivisibility, interdependence and interrelatedness of all human rights and fundamental freedoms and the need for persons with disabilities to be guaranteed their full enjoyment without discrimination,

(d) *Recalling* the International Covenant on Economic, Social and Cultural Rights, the International Covenant on Civil and Political Rights, the International Convention on the Elimination of All Forms of Racial Discrimination, the Convention on the Elimination of All Forms of Discrimination against Women, the Convention against Torture and Other Cruel, Inhuman or Degrading Treatment or Punishment, the Convention on the Rights of the Child, and the International Convention on the Protection of the Rights of All Migrant Workers and Members of Their Families,

(e) *Recognizing* that disability is an evolving concept and that disability results from the interaction between persons with impairments and attitudinal and environmental barriers that hinders their full and effective participation in society on an equal basis with others,

(f) *Recognizing* the importance of the principles and policy guidelines contained in the World Programme of Action concerning Disabled Persons and in the Standard Rules on the Equalization of Opportunities for Persons with Disabilities in influencing the promotion, formulation and evaluation of the policies, plans, programmes and actions at the national, regional and international levels to further equalize opportunities for persons with disabilities,

(g) *Emphasizing* the importance of mainstreaming disability issues as an integral part of relevant strategies of sustainable development,

(h) *Recognizing also* that discrimination against any person on the basis of disability is a violation of the inherent dignity and worth of the human person,

(i) *Recognizing further* the diversity of persons with disabilities,

(j) *Recognizing* the need to promote and protect the human rights of all persons with disabilities, including those who require more intensive support,

(k) *Concerned* that, despite these various instruments and undertakings, persons with disabilities continue to face barriers in their participation as equal members of society and violations of their human rights in all parts of the world,

(l) *Recognizing* the importance of international cooperation for improving the living conditions of persons with disabilities in every country, particularly in developing countries,

(m) *Recognizing* the valued existing and potential contributions made by persons with disabilities to the overall well-being and diversity of their communities, and that the promotion of the full enjoyment by persons with disabilities of their human rights and fundamental freedoms and of full participation by persons with disabilities will result in their enhanced sense of belonging and in significant advances in the human, social and economic development of society and the eradication of poverty,

(n) *Recognizing* the importance for persons with disabilities of their individual autonomy and independence, including the freedom to make their own choices,

(o) *Considering* that persons with disabilities should have the opportunity to be actively involved in decision-making processes about policies and programmes, including those directly concerning them,

(p) *Concerned* about the difficult conditions faced by persons with disabilities who are subject to multiple or aggravated forms of discrimination on the basis of race, colour, sex, language, religion, political or other opinion, national, ethnic, indigenous or social origin, property, birth, age or other status,

(q) *Recognizing* that women and girls with disabilities are often at greater risk, both within and outside the home of violence, injury or abuse, neglect or negligent treatment, maltreatment or exploitation,

(r) *Recognizing* that children with disabilities should have full enjoyment of all human rights and fundamental freedoms on an equal basis with other children, and recalling obligations to that end undertaken by States Parties to the Convention on the Rights of the Child,

(s) *Emphasizing* the need to incorporate a gender perspective in all efforts to promote the full enjoyment of human rights and fundamental freedoms by persons with disabilities,

(t) *Highlighting* the fact that the majority of persons with disabilities live in conditions of poverty, and in this regard recognizing the critical need to address the negative impact of poverty on persons with disabilities,

(u) *Bearing in mind* that conditions of peace and security based on full respect for the purposes and principles contained in the Charter of the United Nations and observance of applicable human rights instruments are indispensable for the full protection of persons with disabilities, in particular during armed conflicts and foreign occupation,

(v) *Recognizing* the importance of accessibility to the physical, social, economic and cultural environment, to health and education and to information and communication, in enabling persons with disabilities to fully enjoy all human rights and fundamental freedoms,

(w) *Realizing* that the individual, having duties to other individuals and to the community to which he or she belongs, is under a responsibility to strive for the promotion and observance of the rights recognized in the International Bill of Human Rights,

(x) *Convinced* that the family is the natural and fundamental group unit of society and is entitled to protection by society and the State, and that persons with disabilities and their family members should receive the necessary protection and assistance to enable families to contribute towards the full and equal enjoyment of the rights of persons with disabilities,

(y) *Convinced* that a comprehensive and integral international convention to promote and protect the rights and dignity of persons with disabilities will make a significant contribution to redressing the profound social disadvantage of persons with disabilities and promote their participation in the civil, political, economic, social and cultural spheres with equal opportunities, in both developing and developed countries,

Have agreed as follows:

Article 1
Purpose

The purpose of the present Convention is to promote, protect and ensure the full and equal enjoyment of all human rights and fundamental freedoms by all persons with disabilities, and to promote respect for their inherent dignity.

Persons with disabilities include those who have long-term physical, mental, intellectual or sensory impairments which in interaction with various barriers may hinder their full and effective participation in society on an equal basis with others.

Article 2
Definitions

For the purposes of the present Convention:

"Communication" includes languages, display of text, Braille, tactile communication, large print, accessible multimedia as well as written, audio, plain-language, human-reader and augmentative and alternative modes, means and formats of communication, including accessible information and communication technology;

"Language" includes spoken and signed languages and other forms of non spoken languages;

"Discrimination on the basis of disability" means any distinction, exclusion or restriction on the basis of disability which has the purpose or effect of impairing or nullifying the recognition, enjoyment or exercise, on an equal basis with others, of all human rights and fundamental freedoms in the political, economic, social, cultural, civil or any other field. It includes all forms of discrimination, including denial of reasonable accommodation;

"Reasonable accommodation" means necessary and appropriate modification and adjustments not imposing a disproportionate or undue burden, where needed in a particular case, to ensure to persons with disabilities the enjoyment or exercise on an equal basis with others of all human rights and fundamental freedoms;

"Universal design" means the design of products, environments, programmes and services to be usable by all people, to the greatest extent possible, without the need for adaptation or specialized design. "Universal design" shall not exclude assistive devices for particular groups of persons with disabilities where this is needed.

Article 3
General principles

The principles of the present Convention shall be:

(a) Respect for inherent dignity, individual autonomy including the freedom to make one's own choices, and independence of persons;

(b) Non-discrimination;

(c) Full and effective participation and inclusion in society;

(d) Respect for difference and acceptance of persons with disabilities as part of human diversity and humanity;

(e) Equality of opportunity;

(f) Accessibility;

(g) Equality between men and women;

(h) Respect for the evolving capacities of children with disabilities and respect for the right of children with disabilities to preserve their identities.

Article 4
General obligations

1. States Parties undertake to ensure and promote the full realization of all human rights and fundamental freedoms for all persons with disabilities without discrimination of any kind on the basis of disability. To this end, States Parties undertake:

(a) To adopt all appropriate legislative, administrative and other measures for the implementation of the rights recognized in the present Convention;

(b) To take all appropriate measures, including legislation, to modify or abolish existing laws, regulations, customs and practices that constitute discrimination against persons with disabilities;

(c) To take into account the protection and promotion of the human rights of persons with disabilities in all policies and programmes;

(d) To refrain from engaging in any act or practice that is inconsistent with the present Convention and to ensure that public authorities and institutions act in conformity with the present Convention;

(e) To take all appropriate measures to eliminate discrimination on the basis of disability by any person, organization or private enterprise;

(f) To undertake or promote research and development of universally designed goods, services, equipment and facilities, as defined in article 2 of the present Convention, which should require the minimum possible adaptation and the least cost to meet the specific needs of a person with disabilities, to promote their availability and use, and to promote universal design in the development of standards and guidelines;

(g) To undertake or promote research and development of, and to promote the availability and use of new technologies, including information and communications technologies, mobility aids, devices and assistive technologies, suitable for persons with disabilities, giving priority to technologies at an affordable cost;

(h) To provide accessible information to persons with disabilities about mobility aids, devices and assistive technologies, including new technologies, as well as other forms of assistance, support services and facilities;

(i) To promote the training of professionals and staff working with persons with disabilities in the rights recognized in this Convention so as to better provide the assistance and services guaranteed by those rights.

2. With regard to economic, social and cultural rights, each State Party undertakes to take measures to the maximum of its available resources and, where needed, within the framework of international cooperation, with a view to achieving progressively the full realization of these rights, without prejudice to those obligations contained in the present Convention that are immediately applicable according to international law.

3. In the development and implementation of legislation and policies to implement the present Convention, and in other decision-making processes concerning issues relating to persons with disabilities, States Parties shall closely consult with and actively involve persons with disabilities, including children with disabilities, through their representative organizations.

4. Nothing in the present Convention shall affect any provisions which are more conducive to the realization of the rights of persons with disabilities and which may be contained in the law of a State Party or international law in force for that State. There shall be no restriction upon or derogation from any of the human rights and fundamental freedoms recognized or existing in any State Party to the present Convention pursuant to law, conventions, regulation or custom on the pretext that the present Convention does not recognize such rights or freedoms or that it recognizes them to a lesser extent.

5. The provisions of the present Convention shall extend to all parts of federal states without any limitations or exceptions.

Article 5
Equality and non-discrimination

1. States Parties recognize that all persons are equal before and under the law and are entitled without any discrimination to the equal protection and equal benefit of the law.

2. States Parties shall prohibit all discrimination on the basis of disability and guarantee to persons with disabilities equal and effective legal protection against discrimination on all grounds.

3. In order to promote equality and eliminate discrimination, States Parties shall take all appropriate steps to ensure that reasonable accommodation is provided.

4. Specific measures which are necessary to accelerate or achieve de facto equality of persons with disabilities shall not be considered discrimination under the terms of the present Convention.

Article 6
Women with disabilities

1. States Parties recognize that women and girls with disabilities are subject to multiple discrimination, and in this regard shall take measures to ensure the full and equal enjoyment by them of all human rights and fundamental freedoms.

2. States Parties shall take all appropriate measures to ensure the full development, advancement and empowerment of women, for the purpose of guaranteeing them the exercise and enjoyment of the human rights and fundamental freedoms set out in the present Convention.

Article 7
Children with disabilities

1. States Parties shall take all necessary measures to ensure the full enjoyment by children with disabilities of all human rights and fundamental freedoms on an equal basis with other children.

2. In all actions concerning children with disabilities, the best interests of the child shall be a primary consideration.

3. States Parties shall ensure that children with disabilities have the right to express their views freely on all matters affecting them, their views being given due weight in accordance with their age and maturity, on an equal basis with other children, and to be provided with disability and age-appropriate assistance to realize that right.

Article 8
Awareness-raising

1. States Parties undertake to adopt immediate, effective and appropriate measures:

(a) To raise awareness throughout society, including at the family level, regarding persons with disabilities, and to foster respect for the rights and dignity of persons with disabilities;

(b) To combat stereotypes, prejudices and harmful practices relating to persons with disabilities, including those based on sex and age, in all areas of life;

(c) To promote awareness of the capabilities and contributions of persons with disabilities.

2. Measures to this end include:

(a) Initiating and maintaining effective public awareness campaigns designed:

(i) To nurture receptiveness to the rights of persons with disabilities;
(ii) To promote positive perceptions and greater social awareness towards persons with disabilities;

(iii) To promote recognition of the skills, merits and abilities of persons with disabilities, and of their contributions to the workplace and the labour market;

(b) Fostering at all levels of the education system, including in all children from an early age, an attitude of respect for the rights of persons with disabilities;

(c) Encouraging all organs of the media to portray persons with disabilities in a manner consistent with the purpose of the present Convention;

(d) Promoting awareness-training programmes regarding persons with disabilities and the rights of persons with disabilities.

Article 9
Accessibility

1. To enable persons with disabilities to live independently and participate fully in all aspects of life, States Parties shall take appropriate measures to ensure to persons with disabilities access, on an equal basis with others, to the physical environment, to transportation, to information and communications, including information and communications technologies and systems, and to other facilities and services open or provided to the public, both in urban and in rural areas. These measures, which shall include the identification and elimination of obstacles and barriers to accessibility, shall apply to, inter alia:

(a) Buildings, roads, transportation and other indoor and outdoor facilities, including schools, housing, medical facilities and workplaces;

(b) Information, communications and other services, including electronic services and emergency services.

2. States Parties shall also take appropriate measures to:

(a) Develop, promulgate and monitor the implementation of minimum standards and guidelines for the accessibility of facilities and services open or provided to the public;

(b) Ensure that private entities that offer facilities and services which are open or provided to the public take into account all aspects of accessibility for persons with disabilities;

(c) Provide training for stakeholders on accessibility issues facing persons with disabilities;

(d) Provide in buildings and other facilities open to the public signage in Braille and in easy to read and understand forms;

(e) Provide forms of live assistance and intermediaries, including guides, readers and professional sign language interpreters, to facilitate accessibility to buildings and other facilities open to the public;

(f) Promote other appropriate forms of assistance and support to persons with disabilities to ensure their access to information;

(g) Promote access for persons with disabilities to new information and communications technologies and systems, including the Internet;

(h) Promote the design, development, production and distribution of accessible information and communications technologies and systems at an early stage, so that these technologies and systems become accessible at minimum cost.

Article 10
Right to life

States Parties reaffirm that every human being has the inherent right to life and shall take all necessary measures to ensure its effective enjoyment by persons with disabilities on an equal basis with others.

Article 11
Situations of risk and humanitarian emergencies

States Parties shall take, in accordance with their obligations under international law, including international humanitarian law and international human rights law, all necessary measures to ensure the protection and safety of persons with disabilities in situations of risk, including situations of armed conflict, humanitarian emergencies and the occurrence of natural disasters.

Article 12
Equal recognition before the law

1. States Parties reaffirm that persons with disabilities have the right to recognition everywhere as persons before the law.

2. States Parties shall recognize that persons with disabilities enjoy legal capacity on an equal basis with others in all aspects of life.

3. States Parties shall take appropriate measures to provide access by persons with disabilities to the support they may require in exercising their legal capacity.

4. States Parties shall ensure that all measures that relate to the exercise of legal capacity provide for appropriate and effective safeguards to prevent abuse in accordance with international human rights law. Such safeguards shall ensure that measures relating to the exercise of legal capacity respect the rights, will and preferences of the person, are free of conflict of interest and undue influence, are proportional and tailored to the person's circumstances, apply for the shortest time possible and are subject to regular review by a competent, independent and impartial authority or judicial body. The safeguards shall be proportional to the degree to which such measures affect the person's rights and interests.

5. Subject to the provisions of this article, States Parties shall take all appropriate and effective measures to ensure the equal right of persons with disabilities to own or inherit property, to control their own financial affairs and to have equal access to bank loans, mortgages and other forms of financial credit, and shall ensure that persons with disabilities are not arbitrarily deprived of their property.

Article 13
Access to justice

1. States Parties shall ensure effective access to justice for persons with disabilities on an equal basis with others, including through the provision of procedural and age-appropriate accommodations, in order to facilitate their effective role as direct and indirect participants, including as witnesses, in all legal proceedings, including at investigative and other preliminary stages.

2. In order to help to ensure effective access to justice for persons with disabilities, States Parties shall promote appropriate training for those working in the field of administration of justice, including police and prison staff.

Article 14
Liberty and security of the person

1. States Parties shall ensure that persons with disabilities, on an equal basis with others:

(a) Enjoy the right to liberty and security of person;

(b) Are not deprived of their liberty unlawfully or arbitrarily, and that any deprivation of liberty is in conformity with the law, and that the existence of a disability shall in no case justify a deprivation of liberty.

2. States Parties shall ensure that if persons with disabilities are deprived of their liberty through any process, they are, on an equal basis with others, entitled to guarantees in accordance with international human rights law and shall be treated in compliance with the objectives and principles of this Convention, including by provision of reasonable accommodation.

Article 15
Freedom from torture or cruel, inhuman or degrading treatment
or punishment

1. No one shall be subjected to torture or to cruel, inhuman or degrading treatment or punishment. In particular, no one shall be subjected without his or her free consent to medical or scientific experimentation.

2. States Parties shall take all effective legislative, administrative, judicial or other measures to prevent persons with disabilities, on an equal basis with others, from being subjected to torture or cruel, inhuman or degrading treatment or punishment.

Article 16
Freedom from exploitation, violence and abuse

1. States Parties shall take all appropriate legislative, administrative, social, educational and other measures to protect persons with disabilities, both within and outside the home, from all forms of exploitation, violence and abuse, including their gender-based aspects.

2. States Parties shall also take all appropriate measures to prevent all forms of exploitation, violence and abuse by ensuring, inter alia, appropriate forms of gender- and age-sensitive assistance and support for persons with disabilities and their families and caregivers, including through the provision of information and education on how to avoid, recognize and report instances of exploitation, violence and abuse. States Parties shall ensure that protection services are age-, gender- and disability-sensitive.

3. In order to prevent the occurrence of all forms of exploitation, violence and abuse, States Parties shall ensure that all facilities and programmes designed to serve persons with disabilities are effectively monitored by independent authorities.

4. States Parties shall take all appropriate measures to promote the physical, cognitive and psychological recovery, rehabilitation and social reintegration of persons with disabilities who become victims of any form of exploitation, violence or abuse, including through the provision of protection services. Such recovery and reintegration shall take place in an environment that fosters the health, welfare, self-respect, dignity and autonomy of the person and takes into account gender- and age-specific needs.

5. States Parties shall put in place effective legislation and policies, including women- and child-focused legislation and policies, to ensure that instances of exploitation, violence and abuse against persons with disabilities are identified, investigated and, where appropriate, prosecuted.

Article 17
Protecting the integrity of the person

Every person with disabilities has a right to respect for his or her physical and mental integrity on an equal basis with others.

Article 18
Liberty of movement and nationality

1. States Parties shall recognize the rights of persons with disabilities to liberty of movement, to freedom to choose their residence and to a nationality, on an equal basis with others, including by ensuring that persons with disabilities:

(a) Have the right to acquire and change a nationality and are not deprived of their nationality arbitrarily or on the basis of disability;

(b) Are not deprived, on the basis of disability, of their ability to obtain, possess and utilize documentation of their nationality or other documentation of identification, or to utilize relevant processes such as immigration proceedings, that may be needed to facilitate exercise of the right to liberty of movement;

(c) Are free to leave any country, including their own;

(d) Are not deprived, arbitrarily or on the basis of disability, of the right to enter their own country.

2. Children with disabilities shall be registered immediately after birth and shall have the right from birth to a name, the right to acquire a nationality and, as far as possible, the right to know and be cared for by their parents.

Article 19
Living independently and being included in the community

States Parties to this Convention recognize the equal right of all persons with disabilities to live in the community, with choices equal to others, and shall take effective and appropriate measures to facilitate full enjoyment by persons with disabilities of this right and their full inclusion and participation in the community, including by ensuring that:

(a) Persons with disabilities have the opportunity to choose their place of residence and where and with whom they live on an equal basis with others and are not obliged to live in a particular living arrangement;

(b) Persons with disabilities have access to a range of in-home, residential and other community support services, including personal assistance necessary to support living and inclusion in the community, and to prevent isolation or segregation from the community;

(c) Community services and facilities for the general population are available on an equal basis to persons with disabilities and are responsive to their needs.

Article 20
Personal mobility

States Parties shall take effective measures to ensure personal mobility with the greatest possible independence for persons with disabilities, including by:

(a) Facilitating the personal mobility of persons with disabilities in the manner and at the time of their choice, and at affordable cost;

(b) Facilitating access by persons with disabilities to quality mobility aids, devices, assistive technologies and forms of live assistance and intermediaries, including by making them available at affordable cost;

(c) Providing training in mobility skills to persons with disabilities and to specialist staff working with persons with disabilities;

(d) Encouraging entities that produce mobility aids, devices and assistive technologies to take into account all aspects of mobility for persons with disabilities.

Article 21
Freedom of expression and opinion, and access to information

States Parties shall take all appropriate measures to ensure that persons with disabilities can exercise the right to freedom of expression and opinion, including the freedom to seek, receive and impart information and ideas on an equal basis with others and through all forms of communication of their choice, as defined in article 2 of the present Convention, including by:

(a) Providing information intended for the general public to persons with disabilities in accessible formats and technologies appropriate to different kinds of disabilities in a timely manner and without additional cost;

(b) Accepting and facilitating the use of sign languages, Braille, augmentative and alternative communication, and all other accessible means, modes and formats of communication of their choice by persons with disabilities in official interactions;

(c) Urging private entities that provide services to the general public, including through the Internet, to provide information and services in accessible and usable formats for persons with disabilities;

(d) Encouraging the mass media, including providers of information through the Internet, to make their services accessible to persons with disabilities;

(e) Recognizing and promoting the use of sign languages.

Article 22
Respect for privacy

1. No person with disabilities, regardless of place of residence or living arrangements, shall be subjected to arbitrary or unlawful interference with his or her privacy, family, home or correspondence or other types of communication or to unlawful attacks on his or her honour and reputation. Persons with disabilities have the right to the protection of the law against such interference or attacks.

2. States Parties shall protect the privacy of personal, health and rehabilitation information of persons with disabilities on an equal basis with others.

Article 23
Respect for home and the family

1. States Parties shall take effective and appropriate measures to eliminate discrimination against persons with disabilities in all matters relating to marriage, family, parenthood and relationships, on an equal basis with others, so as to ensure that:

(a) The right of all persons with disabilities who are of marriageable age to marry and to found a family on the basis of free and full consent of the intending spouses is recognized;

(b) The rights of persons with disabilities to decide freely and responsibly on the number and spacing of their children and to have access to age-appropriate information, reproductive and family planning education are recognized, and the means necessary to enable them to exercise these rights are provided;

(c) Persons with disabilities, including children, retain their fertility on an equal basis with others.

2. States Parties shall ensure the rights and responsibilities of persons with disabilities, with regard to guardianship, wardship, trusteeship, adoption of children or similar institutions, where these concepts exist in national legislation; in all cases the best interests of the child shall be paramount. States Parties shall render appropriate assistance to persons with disabilities in the performance of their child-rearing responsibilities.

3. States Parties shall ensure that children with disabilities have equal rights with respect to family life. With a view to realizing these rights, and to prevent concealment, abandonment, neglect and segregation of children with disabilities, States Parties shall undertake to provide early and comprehensive information, services and support to children with disabilities and their families.

4. States Parties shall ensure that a child shall not be separated from his or her parents against their will, except when competent authorities subject to judicial review determine, in accordance with applicable law and procedures, that such separation is necessary for the best interests of the child. In no case shall a child be separated from parents on the basis of a disability of either the child or one or both of the parents.

5. States Parties shall, where the immediate family is unable to care for a child with disabilities, undertake every effort to provide alternative care within the wider family, and failing that, within the community in a family setting.

Article 24
Education

1. States Parties recognize the right of persons with disabilities to education. With a view to realizing this right without discrimination and on the basis of equal

opportunity, States Parties shall ensure an inclusive education system at all levels and life long learning directed to:

(a) The full development of human potential and sense of dignity and self-worth, and the strengthening of respect for human rights, fundamental freedoms and human diversity;

(b) The development by persons with disabilities of their personality, talents and creativity, as well as their mental and physical abilities, to their fullest potential;

(c) Enabling persons with disabilities to participate effectively in a free society.

2. In realizing this right, States Parties shall ensure that:

(a) Persons with disabilities are not excluded from the general education system on the basis of disability, and that children with disabilities are not excluded from free and compulsory primary education, or from secondary education, on the basis of disability;

(b) Persons with disabilities can access an inclusive, quality and free primary education and secondary education on an equal basis with others in the communities in which they live;

(c) Reasonable accommodation of the individual's requirements is provided;

(d) Persons with disabilities receive the support required, within the general education system, to facilitate their effective education;

(e) Effective individualized support measures are provided in environments that maximize academic and social development, consistent with the goal of full inclusion.

3. States Parties shall enable persons with disabilities to learn life and social development skills to facilitate their full and equal participation in education and as members of the community. To this end, States Parties shall take appropriate measures, including:

(a) Facilitating the learning of Braille, alternative script, augmentative and alternative modes, means and formats of communication and orientation and mobility skills, and facilitating peer support and mentoring;

(b) Facilitating the learning of sign language and the promotion of the linguistic identity of the deaf community;

(c) Ensuring that the education of persons, and in particular children, who are blind, deaf or deafblind, is delivered in the most appropriate languages and modes and means of communication for the individual, and in environments which maximize academic and social development.

4. In order to help ensure the realization of this right, States Parties shall take appropriate measures to employ teachers, including teachers with disabilities, who are qualified in sign language and/or Braille, and to train professionals and staff who work at all levels of education. Such training shall incorporate disability awareness and the use of appropriate augmentative and alternative modes, means and formats of communication, educational techniques and materials to support persons with disabilities.

5. States Parties shall ensure that persons with disabilities are able to access general tertiary education, vocational training, adult education and lifelong learning without discrimination and on an equal basis with others. To this end, States Parties shall ensure that reasonable accommodation is provided to persons with disabilities.

Article 25
Health

States Parties recognize that persons with disabilities have the right to the enjoyment of the highest attainable standard of health without discrimination on the basis of disability. States Parties shall take all appropriate measures to ensure access for persons with disabilities to health services that are gender-sensitive, including health-related rehabilitation. In particular, States Parties shall:

(a) Provide persons with disabilities with the same range, quality and standard of free or affordable health care and programmes as provided to other persons, including in the area of sexual and reproductive health and population-based public health programmes;

(b) Provide those health services needed by persons with disabilities specifically because of their disabilities, including early identification and intervention as appropriate, and services designed to minimize and prevent further disabilities, including among children and older persons;

(c) Provide these health services as close as possible to people's own communities, including in rural areas;

(d) Require health professionals to provide care of the same quality to persons with disabilities as to others, including on the basis of free and informed consent by, inter alia, raising awareness of the human rights, dignity, autonomy and needs of persons with disabilities through training and the promulgation of ethical standards for public and private health care;

(e) Prohibit discrimination against persons with disabilities in the provision of health insurance, and life insurance where such insurance is permitted by national law, which shall be provided in a fair and reasonable manner;

(f) Prevent discriminatory denial of health care or health services or food and fluids on the basis of disability.

Article 26
Habilitation and rehabilitation

1. States Parties shall take effective and appropriate measures, including through peer support, to enable persons with disabilities to attain and maintain maximum independence, full physical, mental, social and vocational ability, and full inclusion and participation in all aspects of life. To that end, States Parties shall organize, strengthen and extend comprehensive habilitation and rehabilitation services and programmes, particularly in the areas of health, employment, education and social services, in such a way that these services and programmes:

(a) Begin at the earliest possible stage, and are based on the multidisciplinary assessment of individual needs and strengths;

(b) Support participation and inclusion in the community and all aspects of society, are voluntary, and are available to persons with disabilities as close as possible to their own communities, including in rural areas.

2. States Parties shall promote the development of initial and continuing training for professionals and staff working in habilitation and rehabilitation services.

3. States Parties shall promote the availability, knowledge and use of assistive devices and technologies, designed for persons with disabilities, as they relate to habilitation and rehabilitation.

Article 27
Work and employment

1. States Parties recognize the right of persons with disabilities to work, on an equal basis with others; this includes the right to the opportunity to gain a living by work freely chosen or accepted in a labour market and work environment that is open, inclusive and accessible to persons with disabilities. States Parties shall safeguard and promote the realization of the right to work, including for those who acquire a disability during the course of employment, by taking appropriate steps, including through legislation, to, inter alia:

(a) Prohibit discrimination on the basis of disability with regard to all matters concerning all forms of employment, including conditions of recruitment, hiring and employment, continuance of employment, career advancement and safe and healthy working conditions;

(b) Protect the rights of persons with disabilities, on an equal basis with others, to just and favourable conditions of work, including equal opportunities and equal remuneration for work of equal value, safe and healthy working conditions, including protection from harassment, and the redress of grievances;

(c) Ensure that persons with disabilities are able to exercise their labour and trade union rights on an equal basis with others;

(d) Enable persons with disabilities to have effective access to general technical and vocational guidance programmes, placement services and vocational and continuing training;

(e) Promote employment opportunities and career advancement for persons with disabilities in the labour market, as well as assistance in finding, obtaining, maintaining and returning to employment;

(f) Promote opportunities for self-employment, entrepreneurship, the development of cooperatives and starting one's own business;

(g) Employ persons with disabilities in the public sector;

(h) Promote the employment of persons with disabilities in the private sector through appropriate policies and measures, which may include affirmative action programmes, incentives and other measures;

(i) Ensure that reasonable accommodation is provided to persons with disabilities in the workplace;

(j) Promote the acquisition by persons with disabilities of work experience in the open labour market;

(k) Promote vocational and professional rehabilitation, job retention and return-to-work programmes for persons with disabilities.

2. States Parties shall ensure that persons with disabilities are not held in slavery or in servitude, and are protected, on an equal basis with others, from forced or compulsory labour.

Article 28
Adequate standard of living and social protection

1. States Parties recognize the right of persons with disabilities to an adequate standard of living for themselves and their families, including adequate food, clothing and housing, and to the continuous improvement of living conditions, and shall take appropriate steps to safeguard and promote the realization of this right without discrimination on the basis of disability.

2. States Parties recognize the right of persons with disabilities to social protection and to the enjoyment of that right without discrimination on the basis of disability, and shall take appropriate steps to safeguard and promote the realization of this right, including measures:

(a) To ensure equal access by persons with disabilities to clean water services, and to ensure access to appropriate and affordable services, devices and other assistance for disability-related needs;

(b) To ensure access by persons with disabilities, in particular women and girls with disabilities and older persons with disabilities, to social protection programmes and poverty reduction programmes;

(c) To ensure access by persons with disabilities and their families living in situations of poverty to assistance from the State with disability-related expenses, including adequate training, counselling, financial assistance and respite care;

(d) To ensure access by persons with disabilities to public housing programmes;

(e) To ensure equal access by persons with disabilities to retirement benefits and programmes.

Article 29
Participation in political and public life

States Parties shall guarantee to persons with disabilities political rights and the opportunity to enjoy them on an equal basis with others, and shall undertake to:

(a) Ensure that persons with disabilities can effectively and fully participate in political and public life on an equal basis with others, directly or through freely chosen representatives, including the right and opportunity for persons with disabilities to vote and be elected, inter alia, by:

(i) Ensuring that voting procedures, facilities and materials are appropriate, accessible and easy to understand and use;

(ii) Protecting the right of persons with disabilities to vote by secret ballot in elections and public referendums without intimidation, and to stand for elections, to effectively hold office and perform all public functions at all levels of government, facilitating the use of assistive and new technologies where appropriate;

(iii) Guaranteeing the free expression of the will of persons with disabilities as electors and to this end, where necessary, at their request, allowing assistance in voting by a person of their own choice;

(b) Promote actively an environment in which persons with disabilities can effectively and fully participate in the conduct of public affairs, without discrimination and on an equal basis with others, and encourage their participation in public affairs, including:

(i) Participation in non-governmental organizations and associations concerned with the public and political life of the country, and in the activities and administration of political parties;

(ii) Forming and joining organizations of persons with disabilities to represent persons with disabilities at international, national, regional and local levels.

Article 30
Participation in cultural life, recreation, leisure and sport

1. States Parties recognize the right of persons with disabilities to take part on an equal basis with others in cultural life, and shall take all appropriate measures to ensure that persons with disabilities:

(a) Enjoy access to cultural materials in accessible formats;

(b) Enjoy access to television programmes, films, theatre and other cultural activities, in accessible formats;

(c) Enjoy access to places for cultural performances or services, such as theatres, museums, cinemas, libraries and tourism services, and, as far as possible, enjoy access to monuments and sites of national cultural importance.

2. States Parties shall take appropriate measures to enable persons with disabilities to have the opportunity to develop and utilize their creative, artistic and intellectual potential, not only for their own benefit, but also for the enrichment of society.

3. States Parties shall take all appropriate steps, in accordance with international law, to ensure that laws protecting intellectual property rights do not constitute an unreasonable or discriminatory barrier to access by persons with disabilities to cultural materials.

4. Persons with disabilities shall be entitled, on an equal basis with others, to recognition and support of their specific cultural and linguistic identity, including sign languages and deaf culture.

5. With a view to enabling persons with disabilities to participate on an equal basis with others in recreational, leisure and sporting activities, States Parties shall take appropriate measures:

(a) To encourage and promote the participation, to the fullest extent possible, of persons with disabilities in mainstream sporting activities at all levels;

(b) To ensure that persons with disabilities have an opportunity to organize, develop and participate in disability-specific sporting and recreational activities and, to this end, encourage the provision, on an equal basis with others, of appropriate instruction, training and resources;

(c) To ensure that persons with disabilities have access to sporting, recreational and tourism venues;

(d) To ensure that children with disabilities have equal access with other children to participation in play, recreation and leisure and sporting activities, including those activities in the school system;

(e) To ensure that persons with disabilities have access to services from those involved in the organization of recreational, tourism, leisure and sporting activities.

Article 31
Statistics and data collection

1. States Parties undertake to collect appropriate information, including statistical and research data, to enable them to formulate and implement policies to give effect to the present Convention. The process of collecting and maintaining this information shall:

(a) Comply with legally established safeguards, including legislation on data protection, to ensure confidentiality and respect for the privacy of persons with disabilities;

(b) Comply with internationally accepted norms to protect human rights and fundamental freedoms and ethical principles in the collection and use of statistics.

2. The information collected in accordance with this article shall be disaggregated, as appropriate, and used to help assess the implementation of States Parties' obligations under the present Convention and to identify and address the barriers faced by persons with disabilities in exercising their rights.

3. States Parties shall assume responsibility for the dissemination of these statistics and ensure their accessibility to persons with disabilities and others.

Article 32
International cooperation

1. States Parties recognize the importance of international cooperation and its promotion, in support of national efforts for the realization of the purpose and objectives of the present Convention, and will undertake appropriate and effective measures in this regard, between and among States and, as appropriate, in partnership with relevant international and regional organizations and civil society, in particular organizations of persons with disabilities. Such measures could include, inter alia:

(a) Ensuring that international cooperation, including international development programmes, is inclusive of and accessible to persons with disabilities;

(b) Facilitating and supporting capacity-building, including through the exchange and sharing of information, experiences, training programmes and best practices;

(c) Facilitating cooperation in research and access to scientific and technical knowledge;

(d) Providing, as appropriate, technical and economic assistance, including by facilitating access to and sharing of accessible and assistive technologies, and through the transfer of technologies.

2. The provisions of this article are without prejudice to the obligations of each State Party to fulfil its obligations under the present Convention.

Article 33
National implementation and monitoring

1. States Parties, in accordance with their system of organization, shall designate one or more focal points within government for matters relating to the implementation of the present Convention, and shall give due consideration to the establishment or designation of a coordination mechanism within government to facilitate related action in different sectors and at different levels.

2. States Parties shall, in accordance with their legal and administrative systems, maintain, strengthen, designate or establish within the State Party, a framework, including one or more independent mechanisms, as appropriate, to promote, protect and monitor implementation of the present Convention. When designating or establishing such a mechanism, States Parties shall take into account the principles relating to the status and functioning of national institutions for protection and promotion of human rights.

3. Civil society, in particular persons with disabilities and their representative organizations, shall be involved and participate fully in the monitoring process.

Article 34
Committee on the Rights of Persons with Disabilities

1. There shall be established a Committee on the Rights of Persons with Disabilities (hereafter referred to as "the Committee"), which shall carry out the functions hereinafter provided.

2. The Committee shall consist, at the time of entry into force of the present Convention, of twelve experts. After an additional sixty ratifications or accessions to the Convention, the membership of the Committee shall increase by six members, attaining a maximum number of eighteen members.

3. The members of the Committee shall serve in their personal capacity and shall be of high moral standing and recognized competence and experience in the field covered by the present Convention. When nominating their candidates, States Parties are invited to give due consideration to the provision set out in article 4.3 of the present Convention.

4. The members of the Committee shall be elected by States Parties, consideration being given to equitable geographical distribution, representation of the different forms of civilization and of the principal legal systems, balanced gender representation and participation of experts with disabilities.

5. The members of the Committee shall be elected by secret ballot from a list of persons nominated by the States Parties from among their nationals at meetings of the Conference of States Parties. At those meetings, for which two thirds of States Parties shall constitute a quorum, the persons elected to the Committee shall be those who obtain the largest number of votes and an absolute majority of the votes of the representatives of States Parties present and voting.

6. The initial election shall be held no later than six months after the date of entry into force of the present Convention. At least four months before the date of each election,

the Secretary-General of the United Nations shall address a letter to the States Parties inviting them to submit the nominations within two months. The Secretary-General shall subsequently prepare a list in alphabetical order of all persons thus nominated, indicating the State Parties which have nominated them, and shall submit it to the States Parties to the present Convention.

7. The members of the Committee shall be elected for a term of four years. They shall be eligible for re-election once. However, the term of six of the members elected at the first election shall expire at the end of two years; immediately after the first election, the names of these six members shall be chosen by lot by the chairperson of the meeting referred to in paragraph 5 of this article.

8. The election of the six additional members of the Committee shall be held on the occasion of regular elections, in accordance with the relevant provisions of this article.

9. If a member of the Committee dies or resigns or declares that for any other cause she or he can no longer perform her or his duties, the State Party which nominated the member shall appoint another expert possessing the qualifications and meeting the requirements set out in the relevant provisions of this article, to serve for the remainder of the term.

10. The Committee shall establish its own rules of procedure.

11. The Secretary-General of the United Nations shall provide the necessary staff and facilities for the effective performance of the functions of the Committee under the present Convention, and shall convene its initial meeting.

12. With the approval of the General Assembly, the members of the Committee established under the present Convention shall receive emoluments from United Nations resources on such terms and conditions as the Assembly may decide, having regard to the importance of the Committee's responsibilities.

13. The members of the Committee shall be entitled to the facilities, privileges and immunities of experts on mission for the United Nations as laid down in the relevant sections of the Convention on the Privileges and Immunities of the United Nations.

Article 35
Reports by States Parties

1. Each State Party shall submit to the Committee, through the Secretary-General of the United Nations, a comprehensive report on measures taken to give effect to its obligations under the present Convention and on the progress made in that regard, within two years after the entry into force of the present Convention for the State Party concerned.

2. Thereafter, States Parties shall submit subsequent reports at least every four years and further whenever the Committee so requests.

3. The Committee shall decide any guidelines applicable to the content of the reports.

4. A State Party which has submitted a comprehensive initial report to the Committee need not, in its subsequent reports, repeat information previously provided. When preparing reports to the Committee, States Parties are invited to consider doing so in an open and transparent process and to give due consideration to the provision set out in article 4.3 of the present Convention.

5. Reports may indicate factors and difficulties affecting the degree of fulfilment of obligations under the present Convention.

Article 36
Consideration of reports

1. Each report shall be considered by the Committee, which shall make such suggestions and general recommendations on the report as it may consider appropriate and shall forward these to the State Party concerned. The State Party may respond with any information it chooses to the Committee. The Committee may request further information from States Parties relevant to the implementation of the present Convention.

2. If a State Party is significantly overdue in the submission of a report, the Committee may notify the State Party concerned of the need to examine the implementation of the present Convention in that State Party, on the basis of reliable information available to the Committee, if the relevant report is not submitted within three months following the notification. The Committee shall invite the State Party concerned to participate in such examination. Should the State Party respond by submitting the relevant report, the provisions of paragraph 1 of this article will apply.

3. The Secretary-General of the United Nations shall make available the reports to all States Parties.

4. States Parties shall make their reports widely available to the public in their own countries and facilitate access to the suggestions and general recommendations relating to these reports.

5. The Committee shall transmit, as it may consider appropriate, to the specialized agencies, funds and programmes of the United Nations, and other competent bodies, reports from States Parties in order to address a request or indication of a need for technical advice or assistance contained therein, along with the Committee's observations and recommendations, if any, on these requests or indications.

Article 37
Cooperation between States Parties and the Committee

1. Each State Party shall cooperate with the Committee and assist its members in the fulfilment of their mandate.

2. In its relationship with States Parties, the Committee shall give due consideration to ways and means of enhancing national capacities for the implementation of the present Convention, including through international cooperation.

Article 38
Relationship of the Committee with other bodies

In order to foster the effective implementation of the present Convention and to encourage international cooperation in the field covered by the present Convention:

(a) The specialized agencies and other United Nations organs shall be entitled to be represented at the consideration of the implementation of such provisions of the present Convention as fall within the scope of their mandate. The Committee may invite the specialized agencies and other competent bodies as it may consider appropriate to provide expert advice on the implementation of the Convention in areas falling within the scope of their respective mandates. The Committee may invite specialized agencies and other United Nations organs to submit reports on the implementation of the Convention in areas falling within the scope of their activities;

(b) The Committee, as it discharges its mandate, shall consult, as appropriate, other relevant bodies instituted by international human rights treaties, with a view to ensuring the consistency of their respective reporting guidelines, suggestions and general recommendations, and avoiding duplication and overlap in the performance of their functions.

Article 39
Report of the Committee

The Committee shall report every two years to the General Assembly and to the Economic and Social Council on its activities, and may make suggestions and general recommendations based on the examination of reports and information received from the States Parties. Such suggestions and general recommendations shall be included in the report of the Committee together with comments, if any, from States Parties.

Article 40
Conference of States Parties

1. The States Parties shall meet regularly in a Conference of States Parties in order to consider any matter with regard to the implementation of the present Convention.

2. No later than six months after the entry into force of the present Convention, the Conference of the States Parties shall be convened by the Secretary-General of the United Nations. The subsequent meetings shall be convened by the Secretary-General of the United Nations biennially or upon the decision of the Conference of States Parties.

Article 41
Depositary

The Secretary-General of the United Nations shall be the depositary of the present Convention.

Article 42
Signature

The present Convention shall be open for signature by all States and by regional integration organizations at United Nations Headquarters in New York as of 30 March 2007.

Article 43
Consent to be bound

The present Convention shall be subject to ratification by signatory States and to formal confirmation by signatory regional integration organizations. It shall be open for accession by any State or regional integration organization which has not signed the Convention.

Article 44
Regional integration organizations

1. "Regional integration organization" shall mean an organization constituted by sovereign States of a given region, to which its member States have transferred competence in respect of matters governed by this Convention. Such organizations shall declare, in their instruments of formal confirmation or accession, the extent of their competence with respect to matters governed by this Convention. Subsequently, they shall inform the depositary of any substantial modification in the extent of their competence.

2. References to "States Parties" in the present Convention shall apply to such organizations within the limits of their competence.

3. For the purposes of article 45, paragraph 1, and article 47, paragraphs 2 and 3, any instrument deposited by a regional integration organization shall not be counted.

4. Regional integration organizations, in matters within their competence, may exercise their right to vote in the Conference of States Parties, with a number of votes equal to the number of their member States that are Parties to this Convention. Such an organization shall not exercise its right to vote if any of its member States exercises its right, and vice versa.

Article 45
Entry into force

1. The present Convention shall enter into force on the thirtieth day after the deposit of the twentieth instrument of ratification or accession.

2. For each State or regional integration organization ratifying, formally confirming or acceding to the Convention after the deposit of the twentieth such instrument, the

Convention shall enter into force on the thirtieth day after the deposit of its own such instrument.

Article 46
Reservations

1. Reservations incompatible with the object and purpose of the present Convention shall not be permitted.

2. Reservations may be withdrawn at any time.

Article 47
Amendments

1. Any State Party may propose an amendment to the present Convention and submit it to the Secretary-General of the United Nations. The Secretary-General shall communicate any proposed amendments to States Parties, with a request to be notified whether they favour a conference of States Parties for the purpose of considering and deciding upon the proposals. In the event that, within four months from the date of such communication, at least one third of the States Parties favour such a conference, the Secretary-General shall convene the conference under the auspices of the United Nations. Any amendment adopted by a majority of two thirds of the States Parties present and voting shall be submitted by the Secretary-General to the General Assembly for approval and thereafter to all States Parties for acceptance.

2. An amendment adopted and approved in accordance with paragraph 1 of this article shall enter into force on the thirtieth day after the number of instruments of acceptance deposited reaches two thirds of the number of States Parties at the date of adoption of the amendment. Thereafter, the amendment shall enter into force for any State Party on the thirtieth day following the deposit of its own instrument of acceptance. An amendment shall be binding only on those States Parties which have accepted it.

3. If so decided by the Conference of States Parties by consensus, an amendment adopted and approved in accordance with paragraph 1 of this article which relates exclusively to articles 34, 38, 39 and 40 shall enter into force for all States Parties on the thirtieth day after the number of instruments of acceptance deposited reaches two thirds of the number of States Parties at the date of adoption of the amendment.

Article 48
Denunciation

A State Party may denounce the present Convention by written notification to the Secretary-General of the United Nations. The denunciation shall become effective one year after the date of receipt of the notification by the Secretary-General.

Article 49
Accessible format

The text of the present Convention shall be made available in accessible formats.

Article 50
Authentic texts

The Arabic, Chinese, English, French, Russian and Spanish texts of the present Convention shall be equally authentic.

In witness thereof the undersigned plenipotentiaries, being duly authorized thereto by their respective Governments, have signed the present Convention.

List of Signatory States of the Convention on the Rights of Persons with Disabilities

As of September 28, 2007

✶ *Signed the Optional Protocol*
✶✶ *Ratified the Convention*

- Algeria ✶
- Andorra ✶
- Antigua y Barbuda ✶
- Argentina ✶
- Armenia ✶
- Australia ✶
- Austria ✶
- Bahrain
- Bangladesh
- Barbados
- Belgium ✶
- Bolivia ✶
- Brazil ✶
- Bulgaria
- Burkina Faso ✶
- Burundi ✶
- Canada
- Cape Verde
- Central African Republic ✶
- Chile ✶
- China
- Colombia
- Comoros
- Congo (Democratic Republic of) ✶
- Costa Rica ✶
- Côte d'Ivoire ✶
- Croatia ✶
- Cuba
- Cyprus ✶
- Czech Republic ✶
- Denmark
- Dominica
  - Dominican Republic ✶
- Ecuador ✶
- Egypt
- El Salvador ✶
- Estonia
- Ethiopia
- Finland ✶
- France
- Gabon
- Germany ✶
- Ghana ✶
- Greece
- Guatemala ✶
- Guinea
- Guyana
- Honduras
- Hungary ✶ ✶
- Iceland ✶
- India
- Indonesia
- Ireland
- Israel
- Italy ✶
- Jamaica ✶ ✶ ✶
- Jordan ✶
- Kenya
- Korea ✶
- Lebanon ✶
- Liberia ✶
- Lithuania ✶
- Luxembourg ✶
- Macedonia
- Madagascar
- Malawi
- Mali ✶
- Malta ✶
- Mauritius
- Mexico ✶
- Moldova ✶
- Montenegro
- Morocco
- Mozambique
- Namibia ✶
- Netherlands
- New Zealand
- Nicaragua
- Niger ✶
- Nigeria ✶
- Norway
- Panama *
- Paraguay ✶
- Peru ✶
- Philippines
- Poland
- Portugal ✶
- Qatar ✶
- Romania
- San Marino ✶
- Senegal ✶
- Seychelles ✶
- Sierra Leone ✶
- Slovakia
- Slovenia ✶
- South Africa ✶
- Spain ✶
- Sri Lanka
- Sudan
- Suriname
- Swaziland
- Sweden ✶
- Syrian Arab Republic ✶
- Tanzania (United Republic of)
- Thailand
- Trinidad and Tobago
- Tunisia
- Turkey
- Uganda ✶
- United Kingdom
- United Republic of Tanzania
- Uruguay
- Vanuatu
- Yemen ✶

- European Union

287

INDEX

A

AABAC 217
AARP 56
Access Israel 219, 238
AccessAbill 218, 252
Accessibility Grades 45
ADA Accessibility Guidelines *See* ADAAG
ADAAG 181
Adaptive Technology Center for the Blind 221
aging population 32, 38, 161
AICTA 151
Air France 2, 12
America Online 121, 187
Americans with Disabilities Act 41, 154, 182, 187, 189, 192
ANEC 13, 166, 167
application programming interface 199
Archimedes 222
ASK-IT ... 131, 132, 133, 134, 135, 136, 223
Assistive Robotic Service Manipulator 224
ATM 45
Automated Teller Machines 42

B

Babinszki
   Tamas Babinszki 13, 77, 89, 176
Ban Ki-Moon 7
bandwidth 46, 47
Bath Institute of Medical Engineering 225
Blanck
   Peter Blanck . 13, 186, 187, 188, 189, 190, 191, 192, 193
BlueEar 226

blueIRIS 227
Bobby 228
body language 67, 68
Boisard
   Marcel Boisard 12
Braille ... 61, 63, 64, 65, 77, 83, 84, 85, 105, 114, 188, 206, 220, 221, 247, 252, 254, 262, 266, 271, 273, 274
Brewer
   Judy Brewer 13, 161

C

Campbell
   Larry Campbell 13, 77
Canon 149, 151
CAPTCHA 119
captioning . 98, 117, 153, 154, 155, 156, 157, 158, 159, 160
Cell C 208
cell phones 42, 126, 156, 209
Chuck Wilsker 52
Conrad N. Hilton Foundation 61
CORA 50, 51, 52, 53, 55, 56
Coraworks 50
Creagan
   Timothy Creagan 13, 181
Creating Opportunities by Recognizing Abilities .... *See* CORA
CSUN 124

D

DAISY 14, 198, 202, 203, 220, 230
DAISY Consortium .. 14, 198, 202, 220, 230
Deaf Alerter 231

Deafblind...................................232
Demographic Imperative...........35
Department of Economic and
    Social Affairs of the United
    Nations....................................37
Design for Inclusion............41, 48
DIADEM..................................233
Digital Planet.......................41, 47
distance learning............42, 46, 74
Dragon Naturally Speaking.......59

E

EASTERN EUROPEAN
    NETWORK ON ACCESS
    TECHNOLOGY ... *See* EENAT
EDeAN.....................................143
EDF........................194, 195, 196
Education for All Children with
    Visual Impairment.................62
Edwards.....................................73
EENAT................................82, 90
e-ISOTIS..........................13, 131
English as a Second Language .47,
    77
ETSI...166
EU .... *See* European Union
European Disability Forum..... *See*
    EDF
European Telecommunications
    Standards Institute...... *See* ETSI
European Union 96, 124, 131, 138,
    139, 144, 194, 195, 233
EZ Access................................235

F

FCC................. 154, 155, 158, 183
Filip
    Ambassador Anda Filip 13, 170,
    210
Fingerhut
    Barry Fingerhut..............13, 108
Firefox............. 121, 122, 123, 124
Floratos
    Nikolaos Floratos.. 13, 131, 136
Forcke

Anne-Rivers Forcke 13, 35, 105
Freedom Scientific 113
Full Access Through Technology
   236

G

Gallegos
    Ambassador Luis Gallegos .. 12,
    13, 16, 21, 23
GameON 237
GameON! 237
GE 91, 92, 93, 95, 96
General Electric... See GE, See GE
Geneva Plan of Action 17
Geneva Principle 17
Giovannini
    Chiara Giovannini.........13, 166
GISA 151
Global Center for Information and
    Communication Technologies
    in Parliament.......................173
Global Industry Standardization
    Association................ *See* GISA
global population 29, 35, 37, 38, 40
Global Work Force Diversity
    Initiative................................32
Goldberg
    Larry Goldberg 13, 99, 153
Gonnot
    Jean-Pierre Gonnot..........13, 23
Google............. 117, 119, 122, 123
Gould
    Martin Gould...................13, 41

H

HDMI......................................156
Hecker
    Frank Hecker................13, 121
Henter
    Ted Henter 13, 113, 115
House of Windows..................238
HP..149
HTML............. 162, 163, 164, 247

I

IBM 2, 13, 35, 100, 105, 106, 114, 118, 122, 123, 149
IBM Easy Web Browsing..........32
IBM Human Ability and Accessibility Center. 13, 32, 35, 105
IITE 72, 73, 75, 76
INCITS.....................................151
Information Technology Industry ....*See* ITI
instant messaging 53, 56
Institute for Information Technologies in Education.. See IITE, See IITE, See IITE
IntelliKeys.................................59
InterNational Committee for Information Technology Standards.................*See* INCITS
International Organization for Standardization ....*See* ISO
Internet ... 2, 13, 25, 52, 53, 55, 56, 64, 84, 116, 117, 119, 121, 125, 126, 127, 128, 129, 130, 171, 173, 174, 187, 188, 189, 192, 207, 228, 240, 253, 258, 267, 271
Internet Explorer 121
Internet Speech........ 126, 128, 129
Inter-Parliamentary Union *See* IPU
Ipeleng Bogopane-Zulu
     Hendrietta Ipeleng Bogopane-Zulu 13, 205
IPU 170, 171, 172, 173
IQ67
ISO 147
ITI......................................149, 151

J

Jaws............................. 13, 78, 113
JAWS 59, 113, 114, 200, 207
JTC1 .... 147, 151, 166

K

KADO ....*See* Korea Agency for Digital Opportunity
Keller, Helen 60
Khan
     Emdad Khan 13, 125
     Sarbuland Khan...............14, 16
Korea Agency for Digital Opportunity and Promotion ...2, 66
Kotsik
     Boris Kotsik 14, 72
Kumar
     Preety Kumar 14, 91
Kurzweil.....................................64

L

Leblois
     Axel Leblois....................11, 14
Léon..57
     René Léon 14
Linux 100, 122

M

Mac OS X................................122
Madhusudan
     CN Madhusudan 12
Mahidol University 83
Manocha
     Dipendra Manocha........14, 198
MATILDAH.............................239
McCabe
     Emilie McCabe 14, 28
medical model 37, 38, 39, 40
Mejia
     Alex Mejia 13
mental disorders 69
Microsoft.... 57, 59, 100, 114, 122, 123, 149, 151, 193, 238, 246
Millennium Development Goals 16, 18, 20, 24, 62
Mobile Care.............................240
Morris-Sambur

Ilene Morris-Sambur 14, 50, 53, 54, 55
Mozilla Foundation ... 13, 118, 121
MTN 208
Mugunghwa Electronics 241
multimedia 198, 203, 230, 245, 262
MySpace 54, 118

N

National Council on Disability . 13, 41
National Federation of the Blind
.... 92, 187, 193
NCD 41, 46
Neater Eater 243
Netscape 121

O

OCR 200, 204
OHCHR 171
ON-NET 83, 85, 87
Open Society Institute 80, 82
open source . 97, 98, 121, 122, 124, 203, 220
Optical Character Recognition *See* OCR
Optional Protocol ... 210, 211, 213, 287
Oracle 151
Overbrook .. 13, 77, 78, 79, 80, 81, 82, 83, 85, 86, 87, 89, 90
Overbrook International Program
See Overbrook, See Overbrook, See Overbrook, See Overbrook, See Overbrook, See Overbrook, See Overbrook
Overbrook School for Blind 77
OVERBROOK-NIPPON NETWORK ON EDUCATIONAL TECHOLOGY ..... *See* ON-NET

P

Paciello 14, 98

Michael Paciello 98
Panasonic 149
Park
SukJa Park 14, 66
Park, Sukja 66
Partnership in Opportunities for Employment through Technology in the Americas *See* POETA
PDA 42, 126, 223
PEBBLES 244
PEN-International 245
Perkins Braillers 61
Perkins School for the Blind 14, 60, 61, 62
Personal Digital Assistant 42
Personal digital assistants *See* PDA
phones 43, 46, 125, 235, 240
Pictograph symbols 69
Placencia Porrero
Immaculada Placiencia Porrero
.... 12, 14, 138
POETA 14, 57, 58, 59, 246
Pride Industries 56

R

ratification 23, 172, 210, 211, 212, 213, 285
Raytheon 56
Recaptcha.net 119
RoboBraille 247
Rothstein
Steven Rothstein 14, 60
Royal National Institute for the Blind 248

S

Salaets
Ken Salaets 14, 149
Samsung 241
SAP 151, 157
SAPI 200
screen magnifiers 118, 123, 124
search engine optimization 117

Section 255 of the
  Telecommunications ... 103, 183
Section 508. 13, 90, 103, 110, 116,
  129, 141, 155, 176, 177, 179,
  182, 183, 184, 228
Sightsavers Dolphin Pen 249
social model of disability 39, 40
Speech Application Programming
  Interface .... *See* SAPI
Sullivan, Anne 60

T

Talking Tins 251
Tamas Babinszki 88
T-Base Communications with
  Vision Australia 252
TechShare 2
Tedoff
  Pauley Tedoff 14
TEITAC 103, 147, 183, 184
TelCoa 52
TELCOA 52
Telecommunications and
  Electronic and Information
  Technology Advisory
  Committee .... 147, 183, *See*
  TEITAC
television 151, 153, 154, 157, 159,
  160, 278
televisions 42
telework 50, 51, 52, 53, 56
Telework Coalition 52
Text to Speech 199
Thailand Association of the Blind
  85
The Signing Web Project 253
The Trust for the Americas 57, 58,
  246
Todd Arnold 53
Tokareva
  Natalia 72
  Natalia Tokareva 14
Trackballs 58
Trekker 254
Trinity College of Music 255

Tsaran
  Victor Tsaran 14, 116
TV 54, 153, 155, 157, 224, 240

U

U.S. Access Board 181, 183
U.S. Senate 41
UN Washington Group on
  Disability Statistics 39
UNDESA 171, 173
UNESCAP 202
UNESCO 14, 19, 72, 75, 221
UNFPA 19
universal design 18, 45, 46, 48,
  186, 189, 191, 263

V

Vardakastanis
  Yannis Vardakastanis.... 14, 194
Vaughn
  John Vaughn 12
video description 157, 158, 159,
  160
video search 117
Vodacom 208
Voice I/O 99
voice recognition 42, 56, 59, 98,
  99, 118

W

W3C . 13, 105, 106, 116, 118, 161,
  163, 164, 165, 166, 198
WAI .... *See* Web Accessibility
  Initiative
Walgreens 56
Walter Reed Army Hospital 51
Web Accessibility Initiative 13,
  106, 161, 162, 166
West
  Frances West 13, 80, 192
WGBH 13, 153, 155, 156, 157
Wheelchairnet.org 256
wiseDX 257
World Bank . 30, 35, 36, 37, 39, 85
WWAAC 258

X

XML 162, 163

Y

Yahoo . 14, 79, 116, 117, 118, 119,
122, 123, 127
Yamada

Hajime Yamada 14, 145

Yonsei Rehabilitation School ... 66,
71
YouTube 118

Z

Zukang
Sha Zukang 15

www.ingramcontent.com/pod-product-compliance
Lightning Source LLC
Chambersburg PA
CBHW051225050326
40689CB00007B/807